Also by Vic Marks

The Somerset County Cricket Scrapbook
Marks Out of XI
The T.C.C.B. Guide to Better Cricket

The Ultimate One-day Cricket Match

Your chance to captain England in the first cricket adventure game

Vic Marks & Robin Drake

Heinemann Kingswood

Heinemann Kingswood
Michelin House, 81 Fulham Road, London SW3 6RB

LONDON MELBOURNE AUCKLAND

First published 1988

0 434 98157 5

Typeset by Rowland Phototypesetting Ltd
Bury St Edmunds, Suffolk
Printed and bound in Great Britain by
Richard Clay Ltd, Bungay, Suffolk

CONTENTS

For

Amy
Anna
Emily
Jessica
Joanna
Rosie
and
Wendy

The authors and publisher would like to thank Patrick Eagar and Adrian Murrell for the use of their phctographs, on the following pages:

Patrick Eagar	34, 53, 55, 57, 75, 79, 83, 121, 128, 131
Adrian Murrell/ Allsport	12–21, 26–33, 35, 36, 59, 61, 65, 71, 77, 101, 107, 141, 145, 151, 153, 155, 168

This book gives you a chance to lead England to glorious victory in a one-day international against the Rest of the World at Lord's, albeit from your living room armchair. It is not complicated to read. Simply start at page one and then obey the instructions that follow the options you are offered from page 48–9 onwards. It is rather more difficult to win, however. Good Luck.

INTRODUCTION

If the news was something of a surprise to you, it completely stunned the rest of the country.

On Wednesday a buff-coloured envelope, postmarked London, landed innocently on your doormat. Bleary-eyed and with no great enthusiasm you opened the envelope and out dropped a white invitation card; probably another party or a wedding, you mused with mild, sleepy anticipation. Picking it up you read the following:

> The Test and County Cricket Board Selection Committee invite you to be available to captain England against the Rest of the World at Lord's . . . RSVP the Secretary of the TCCB (Conditions of Acceptance and Notes and Instructions for International Matches attached).

Yes, this could definitely be categorised as a 'surprise'. Being a keen cricket follower, you realised that over the years the English selectors had placed far greater emphasis upon 'leadership qualities' than their overseas counterparts, who tend to pick the best eleven and let them get on with it. Indeed you had often wondered how many Test matches Mike Brearley would have played if he had been born in Adelaide rather than Harrow. None the less whilst you quietly believed yourself to possess a shrewd cricket brain as well as an ability to motivate those around you, it still came as a bit of a shock that the English selectors were so well aware of these undoubted qualities of yours.

Inside the envelope, typed on yellow paper, were the Conditions of Acceptance and Notes and Instructions. There were eighteen items, the first of which was 'Acceptance'. It read:

> You are requested to inform the secretary of the TCCB at Lord's by telephone or telegram immediately whether:
> a) you are completely fit
> b) you are available
> c) you require hotel accommodation
> d) you accept the invitation on the conditions laid down by the TCCB

e) you require a cap and sweaters (sizes must be given).

After two seconds' thought you decided to answer 'yes' to all these queries though it did occur to you that it was probably more accurate to say that you weren't suffering from any injuries rather than that you were 'completely fit'. Flicking through the document you stopped at item 4 – 'Assembly on the Ground':

> Since most members of the team are likely to be playing for their counties on the day before the match, you are expected to report to the Chairman of Selectors at the hotel as early as reasonably possible . . . The team will be expected to report at the ground at 9.45 a.m.

You rushed past 'Remuneration and Travelling Expenses' – who cares about money at a time like this? – stopping only briefly at 'Complimentary Tickets', where you learnt that you are entitled to four. Problems there. Item 11 informed you how much insurance cover you are entitled to in the event of any calamity ranging from death to the loss of your little toe. How thoughtful. But such details didn't excite you too much, nor did 'Advertising on Cricket Clothes', 'Dress' and 'Turn-out' or even 'Prize Money'. However, captaining England did.

The next twenty-four hours were chaotic. A constant barrage of phone calls from press reporters, who spoke to you as if you were a lifelong friend who had just returned from Papua New Guinea. At first you were flattered and amused by their attentions, but after the tenth interview you were yearning for some peace to collect your thoughts and to think about the challenges that lay ahead. None the less you allowed yourself the luxury of buying a selection of the national papers the next morning. The *Times*'s back-page headline, 'Unprecedented choice of captain by English selectors', provided a stark contrast with some of the tabloids – 'Raw rookie recruited to wrestle with Rest of World'; and underneath, 'Inside – Twenty things you didn't know about England's new skipper'. You noticed with surprise that they had got both your height and weight wrong. Making a rare contribution to *The World at One* – his first since the assassination of Mrs Gandhi – Christopher Martin-Jenkins expressed surprise and a qualified approval of the selection; he believed that there was a lot to be said for the return of the amateur captain, though he questioned whether a Lord's one-day showpiece was the best occasion to introduce him. Interest in England's match against the Rest of the World had already been running high, but now it was at fever pitch.

Meticulously you packed your cricket bag plus a blazer and your club tie and set off for the Westmoreland Hotel, which is no more than a lofted straight drive from the Nursery End at Lord's. On arrival you were taken aback when the smiling hotel receptionist recognised you and immediately arranged for your baggage to be whisked up to your single room. In the foyer you bumped into the Chairman of Selectors. After a few minutes of small talk the Chairman declared that he was 'certain that you are the right man for the job' and he wished you good luck. He added that he had taken the liberty of having a dossier compiled outlining the capabilities of the players on both sides as well as a few thoughts on 60-over matches. Handing it over he hoped it might be of some value and he looked forward to seeing you in the morning. Clutching the dossier under your right arm, you made your way eagerly up to your room, thinking that it might be a good idea to spend a while studying it.

'My God, look what they've sent me,' was A. C. MacLaren's famous reaction to the side that the selectors chose before the fourth Test at Manchester in 1902. However, looking through the ten names listed in the dossier to accompany you on to the field the next day, you were satisfied that the selectors had done a good job this time. Anxious to discover any detail that might enable you to captain the side more effectively, you turned to the profiles of your team, beginning with the opening batsmen.

THE ENGLAND XI

Graham Alan Gooch

(Essex)

BORN:

23 July 1953

Leytonstone, Essex

TEST RECORD:

Bat: 59 matches; 3,746 runs; 196 h.s.; 37.08 average

Bwl: 59 matches; 13 wickets; 2–12 b.b.; 42.00 average

ONE-DAY INT:

Bat: 52 matches; 1,792 runs; 129* h.s.; 37.33 average

Bwl: 52 matches; 19 wickets; 2–12 b.b.; 44.05 average

After a catastrophic start to his Test career (he began with a pair at Lord's against the 1975 Australians) he has become one of the most dominant opening batsmen in the world. He has an excellent record against the awesome pace attack of the West Indies; he opted to meet fire with fire and such an approach suited his no-nonsense, upright style. He's just as likely to be dismissed by a gentle swinger like Roger Binny as by Malcolm Marshall. At Essex he has played a vital role in their one-day successes; if Gooch plays well they invariably win.

His bowling may come in handy, if the pitch is slow or the atmosphere allows the ball to swing. He bowls at a gentle medium pace and can swing the ball either way; and he's unlikely to panic in a crisis; however, he is not likely to strike terror into opposition batsmen, either.

He is a fine catcher, whether in the slips or the outfield. Even though he often trains with West Ham in the winter, he's not quite as nimble around the boundary as he used to be.

Early in his England career he was nicknamed 'Zap' or 'Zapata' by Brearley but now he answers more readily to the more mundane cry of 'Goochie'. He's an excellent mimic and once reduced his colleagues to fits of laughter towards the end of a Test match by breaking down when doing his impersonation of Chris Old bowling. Apparently he's the first bowler to bowl both right- and left-handed in a Test match (imitating Dilip Doshi this time). We'd prefer him not to emulate this feat in a one-day international.

Charles William Jeffrey Athey

(Yorkshire & Gloucestershire)

BORN:
27 July 1957
Middlesbrough

TEST RECORD:
Bat: 17 matches; 722 runs; 123 h.s.; 24.89 average
Bwl: has not bowled

ONE-DAY INT:
Bat: 20 matches; 607 runs; 142* h.s.; 31.94 average
Bwl: has not bowled

At the crease there is an uncanny resemblance to Geoff Boycott; his flannels and shirt immaculately pressed, his pads whitened, his Slazenger bat lovingly sandpapered. In fact his stance and his strokeplay are often reminiscent of Boycott as well, which is hardly surprising since Bill spent his formative years watching him, sometimes from the other end. However, enough is enough and in 1984 he moved down to Gloucester, where he has finally started to fulfil the promise that the journalists, always on the look-out for aspiring young Yorkshiremen for the England team, first spotted in 1977. Like Gooch's, his England career started disastrously, but his steady performances in Australia in 1986/7 must have enhanced his confidence. Athey has plenty of natural flair but, like any self respecting Yorkshireman, is a little reluctant to display it especially if risks are attached. Anyone who witnessed his 142 not out against the New Zealanders at Manchester in a Texaco Trophy match will need no convincing of his potential. When he lets himself go, he is a dangerous batsman.

He has proven to be an excellent fielder in the mid-wicket/cover region for England, taking many catches and effecting several run-outs during the triumphant winter of 1986/7. However, a nagging arm injury has prevented him from throwing the ball with any power over the last two years.

Athey is as reliable as Tetley bitter, with his short back and sides, a reassuring sight for any captain. Whatever the circumstances he'll keep grafting for you, even though he may complain about the wicket. Like many openers before him he's yet to come across the perfect batting wicket.

David Ivon Gower

(Leicestershire)

BORN:
1 April 1957
Tunbridge Wells

TEST RECORD:
Bat: 96 matches; 6,789 runs; 215 h.s.; 44.66 average
Bwl: 96 matches; 1 wicket; 1–1 b.b.; 20.00 average

ONE-DAY INT:
Bat: 102 matches; 2,905 runs; 158 h.s.; 31.92 average
Bwl: has not taken any wickets

The noted wit and housewife, Frances Edmonds, once observed that it would be 'difficult for him to be more laid back without being actually comatose'. True, David Gower has an unusual sense of perspective for an international cricketer; he realises that there are other things in life apart from cricket, but don't let that fool you into thinking that he doesn't care. Nothing could be further from the truth.

It amazes us how often the press have urged us to drop Gower. His record bears comparison with any of the post-war greats and only five English batsmen in history have scored more runs in Test cricket than he has. The problem is that he often looks lazy and casual when he's dismissed, just as he looks lazy and casual when he strokes the ball through the covers for four. Don't let anyone try to change that or even complain about it. He is an excellent fielder in the cover/mid-wicket region but like Bill Athey he's lost his throwing arm, which is why the sight of David sprinting back from the boundary with the ball in his hand and a sheepish grin on his face has become familiar. Someday soon the batsmen will run. If you opt to bowl him, we will assume that the match has already been decided; it is embarrassing that such a gifted cricketer should bowl such filth.

David has skippered England on twenty-two occasions and so can be guaranteed to be helpful and supportive. If you win the match he will not need much persuading to share a glass or two of champagne (provided it is of sufficient quality). If you lose he will probably be happy to accept the odd glass by way of consolation.

Allan Joseph Lamb
(Northants)

BORN:
20 June 1954
Langebaanweg, S. Africa

TEST RECORD:
Bat: 51 matches; 2,644 runs; 137* h.s.; 32.64 average
Bwl: 51 matches; 1 wicket; 1–6 b.b.; 23.00 average

ONE-DAY INT:
Bat: 68 matches; 2,315 runs; 118 h.s.; 41.33 average
Bwl: has not bowled

Even though he has played almost fifty Test matches for England, he has recently been regarded as something of a one-day specialist. On two memorable occasions he has turned almost certain defeat into improbable victory – against the Australians in Sydney in February 1987 and against the West Indies during the World Cup. Obviously he enjoys the cut and thrust of 'instant cricket', but then he enjoys just about everything he does. He has an unquenchable thirst for life so don't expect his corner of the dressing room to be too peaceful. Allan is rarely still for more than thirty seconds and rarely quiet for more than ten. He has a highly developed sense of fun, which usually keeps those around him amused. One of his favourite ruses is to lock the umpires in their room just before it is time for play to start. We'd be grateful if you could avoid this happening tomorrow. His style of batting is ideally suited to the 60-over game and he has become extremely adept at pacing his innings. However watch his running between the wickets; he can be a trifle unreliable.

Allan is one of your best all-round fielders and towards the end of the innings is probably best employed on the boundary. He has a strong, accurate arm, a good pair of hands and is a swift runner despite having such short legs.

If you are feeling energetic why not spend an evening with him? However we suggest that you wait until after the game before you do so.

We suggest that you should bat at no. 5.

Ian Terence Botham

(Somerset & Worcestershire)

BORN:

24 November 1955
Heswall, Cheshire

TEST RECORD:

Bat: 94 matches; 5,057 runs; 208 h.s.; 34.87 average
Bwl: 95 matches; 373 wickets; 8–34 b.b.; 27.86 average

ONE-DAY INT:

Bat: 95 matches; 1,693 runs; 72 h.s.; 22.57 average
Bwl: 95 matches; 116 wickets; 4–56 b.b.; 29.29 average

A cricketing colossus. The W.G. of the modern era. 'The greatest match-winner the game has ever known,' according to Mike Brearley in 1985. It would be surprising if you were not a little intimidated by the prospect of captaining him. However, since Botham's reign as England captain ended in 1981 he has given his full support to all those that have followed. There is no reason why he shouldn't do the same for you. Now that he is the wrong side of thirty his batting is more likely to change the course of a game than his bowling. When he's in full cry, he can be devastating and it makes sense to give him as much of the strike as possible; so, if you bat with him, be prepared to run a few sharp singles at the end of the over. Recently his bowling has become less explosive and less ambitious and in fact more effective in limited-over cricket. He no longer attempts to blast out a wicket every ball, unconcerned by the number of runs conceded; now he has reduced his pace, aims to bowl a line and length and to frustrate the batsmen unless he gets bored or incensed. It's less fun but more realistic. He is an outstanding fieldsman anywhere. We can't recall him dropping an outfield catch.

This match should represent a new challenge and in cricketing terms there aren't many left for Ian so we expect him to be highly motivated. One of his problems in recent years has been 'How do you follow Headingley, Edgbaston, Old Trafford 1981?' It is not possible.

We don't think it a particularly good idea to try to stamp your authority with a curfew on the night before the match. In our experience he often plays better after the occasional glass of lager.

Paul Rupert Downton

(Kent & Middlesex)

BORN:
4 April 1957
Farnborough, Kent

TEST RECORD:
Bat: 27 matches; 701 runs; 74 h.s.; 19.47 average
Bwl: has not bowled: 61 catches & 5 stumpings

ONE-DAY INT:
Bat: 17 matches; 193 runs; 44* h.s.; 19.30 average
Bwl: has not bowled: 12 catches & 2 stumpings

Paul was plucked from Exeter University to tour as Bob Taylor's understudy in 1977. He had to wait until 1980 for his first Test appearance; since then he has played twenty-six more times for England, threatening to become an automatic selection like his mentor Alan Knott, but never quite achieving this happy state of affairs. He's not a particularly pretty or stylish 'keeper, but he makes very few mistakes.

Even though he is by nature a shy, gently spoken character he takes his role as the linchpin of the fielding side seriously. He is forever urging his fielders to greater effort and encouraging his bowlers, just as the good wicketkeeper should. Once he has returned to the dressing room he is much quieter; if you want to be able to hear yourself think we suggest that you change closer to him than Allan Lamb.

When he began his county career his batting was very stodgy; now he is one of the most effective 'keeper/batsmen in the country. Again pragmatism rather than elegance is his prime consideration. In one-day cricket he is capable of clever improvisations, often involving delicate sweeps and chips over the infield. Indeed he has occasionally opened the batting for England in one-day internationals.

Paul is totally reliable and committed to the team. Another generation would have regarded him as the type of fellow 'you would choose to go tiger shooting with'. What higher compliment is there?

John Ernest Emburey

(Middlesex)

BORN:
20 August 1952
Peckham, London

TEST RECORD:
Bat: 46 matches; 1,027 runs; 75 h.s.; 19.01 average
Bwl: 46 matches; 115 wickets; 7–78 b.b.; 33.52 average

ONE-DAY INT:
Bat: 36 matches; 295 runs; 34 h.s.; 14.75 average
Bwl: 36 matches; 42 wickets; 4–37 b.b.; 32.28 average

If elegance is not Paul Downton's prime consideration when batting, then John Emburey doesn't consider it at all. Yet he is a treat to watch at the crease simply because you never know what he's going to do next. He has in his armoury a strange collection of shovels, scoops and swats that have driven the best bowlers wild. His falling sweep is reminiscent (though only slightly) of Rohan Kanhai's and he is prepared to play it to almost any ball. In fact such unorthodoxy has made him a feared late-order batsman in one-day cricket. Despite having no back-lift and owing nothing to the *MCC Coaching Manual* he can hit the ball immense distances, once managing six sixes in seven balls when playing for Western Province in South Africa.

However he is selected primarily for his bowling; here he pays more attention to the textbooks, possessing a fine off-spinner's action. He is a niggardly bowler, reluctant to experiment or risk too much, qualities that are often admirable in a one-day game. He likes to prey on a batsman's patience, to tie him down and force him into error rather than to bowl the unplayable ball every time he ambles up to the wicket. He has a strong arm, which means that he is capable of bowling very quickly for a spinner. Sometimes he has been effective at the end of a one-day innings.

He is an excellent fieldsman, and he possesses a sharp cricket brain as well as an intimate knowledge of Lord's Cricket Ground.

His sense of humour can unquestionably be classified as 'dry'. Your first impressions may lead you to think that 'Embers' is a trifle over-keen to emphasise the bleaker side of things. In fact he is not being quite as serious as you first imagine.

Neil Alan Foster

(Essex)

BORN:

6 May 1962
Colchester

TEST RECORD:

Bat: 19 matches; 220 runs; 29 h.s.; 9.16 average

Bwl: 19 matches; 54 wickets; 8–107 b.b.; 33.68 average

ONE-DAY INT:

Bat: 34 matches; 96 runs; 24 h.s.; 8.72 average

Bwl: 34 matches; 36 wickets; 3–29 b.b.; 34.50 average

Neil Foster is a man in a hurry. For three or four years he found himself on the fringes of the England XI, often in the touring side but not the Test team. This is a frustrating time and Neil found it more frustrating than most. Now he is more of a fixture in the England side after an excellent summer in 1987 and is therefore more relaxed.

He possesses many of the attributes necessary for a top fast bowler; a short rhythmical run-up, followed by a flowing loose-limbed action; his arm is usually high; he bowls from close to the stumps and he can swing the ball away from the batsman. In the past he has been a little impetuous in one-day games and it is only fairly recently that he has become a regular in the Essex Sunday team.

His batting improves every year and by the end of his career we think that he may end up as a genuine all-rounder. Also, he is an excellent boundary fielder with good hands and a strong arm. He is a forthright character quite prepared to express his views on the game without any self-consciousness or indeed self-doubt. So don't assume that because he is a fast bowler with a broad country accent he can be easily manipulated. He is too intelligent for that.

Philippe Henri Edmonds

(Middlesex)

BORN:

8 March 1951
Lusaka, N. Rhodesia

TEST RECORD:

Bat: 51 matches; 875 runs; 64 h.s.; 17.50 average
Bwl: 51 matches; 125 wickets; 7–66 b.b.; 34.18 average

ONE-DAY INT:

Bat: 29 matches; 116 runs; 20 h.s.; 10.54 average
Bwl: 29 matches; 26 wickets; 3–39 b.b.; 37.11 average

Some might call this a risky selection since Phil is no longer a professional, but we have decided to go for class. We feel that if Phil is allowed to fulfil his stated ambition of playing as an amateur he is bound to perform well. Also we felt it desirable that you should have a balanced attack at your disposal. I trust there's no further need to justify his selection; we've already spent hours in the past justifying his omission from England teams.

Temperamentally Edmonds provides an obvious contrast with John Emburey. Edmonds, the bowler, can be impatient and eager to experiment with different types of delivery as well as unorthodox field placements. This can sometimes unsettle the best of batsmen but we do urge you not to let him bowl any of his wrist-spinners; these have yet to be successful or economical in any type of first-class cricket.

In the field he is a fine catcher, though less speedy than when he represented Cambridge University as a back-row forward. As for his batting, it is hard now to believe that he has opened the innings for Middlesex on several occasions. However, he's still capable of twenty-minute gems.

Phil is an independent fellow; he probably won't lead the community singing in the showers, but there's no doubt that he will be anxious to impress in a game of this importance. Apart from anything else it's good for business. Don't be surprised if Phil doesn't spend the entire England innings avidly watching the cricket. If you need him he's more likely to be on the phone. Try to keep on the right side of his wife, unless you're prepared to take some stick on 'Wogan'.

Graham Roy Dilley

(Kent & Worcestershire)

BORN:
18 May 1959
Dartford

TEST RECORD:
Bat: 30 matches; 391 runs; 56 h.s.; 13.48 average
Bwl: 30 matches; 99 wickets; 6–154 b.b.; 30.02 average

ONE-DAY INT:
Bat: 34 matches; 114 runs; 31* h.s.; 11.40 average
Bwl: 34 matches; 45 wickets; 4–23 b.b.; 26.26 average

On his day perhaps the quickest of the English bowlers, he has the priceless ability to swing the ball away from the right-handed batsman as well. A major handicap in his development has been that he is more injury prone than many of his colleagues; his bowling action places heavy stress on his body and he once stated that he is 'resigned to the fact that I may end up in a wheelchair any time'. You may deduce from this that he is not one of the world's greatest optimists.

For a fast bowler he's a gentle soul, who lacks the innate confidence of a Trueman or even his new county colleague, Neal Radford, so do everything you can to keep his confidence high. Once this is achieved he can be a match-winning bowler. On the tour of Australia in 1986/7 his contributions were decisive in the one-day successes as well as in the Test matches. He has played one memorable innings for England in partnership with Botham in the Headingley Test of 1981, but recently has seemed quite content to come out to bat 'just before the roller'. He is a reliable outfielder. He's nicknamed 'Picca'. We'll leave you to work that one out. You don't need to be an Einstein or a Brearley to do so.

All very useful stuff, but no substitute for meeting your team in the flesh. That would have to wait until the following morning. Before examining the opposition, you decided to see what the dossier had to offer on the 60-over game.

THE RULES

The match is sixty overs per side and no bowler is allowed to bowl more than twelve overs. Otherwise the normal laws of cricket apply except that four fielders must be within an inner circle at all times. This law was implemented in England about half a dozen years ago and has greatly enhanced the game. To avoid any confusion we'll quote it in full:

'At the instant of delivery a minimum of four fieldsmen (plus the bowler and the wicket-keeper) must be within an area bounded by two semicircles centred on each middle stump (each with a radius of 30 yards) and joined by a parallel line on each side of the pitch. In the event of an infringement, the square-leg umpire shall call "No-Ball". The fielding circle should be marked by painted white "dots" at five-yard intervals.'

We hope that clarifies the situation.

Sixty overs is a long time, probably as long as any match that you have previously played in, so don't become too obsessed by 'limited-over tactics' too early in the innings.

When your team is batting remember to stress the importance of having wickets in hand during the last few overs. At the halfway stage it is generally much better to be 100–2 than 130–5. If a recognised batsman is still in with half a dozen overs left he can often cause mayhem, especially since the introduction of the inner circle.

When you take to the field the emphasis during the opening overs should be to dismiss rather than to contain the batsmen. In the long run taking wickets is the best method of slowing the run-rate. So most captains try to keep their attacking fieldsmen for as long as possible. It is up to you to decide whether the batsman is more likely to be caught at second slip because the ball is swinging or at mid-wicket because a defensive ring of fielders has forced him to try something risky. It is, you will discover, a difficult balance to achieve and often there are no right answers. Of course we have every confidence in your ability to stay cool under pressure and to think quickly – that is why we picked you –

but we feel that we should warn you that the last few overs in the field can be complete chaos. Adjustments may be necessary every ball and there will be no time to consult your colleagues. However, don't forget that even world-class players feel the pressure induced by a tight finish and a grand occasion; it's just that they disguise this fact better than most. We should also remind you that the team will be penalised for slow over-rates and one thing modern professionals dislike is forfeiting some of their hard earned pay because of a dithering captain.

Good luck. Here are a few thoughts about the oppo. On paper they don't look a bad side.

It was difficult to disagree with this assessment of your opponents. With sweaty palms you turned the page in search of more guidance and summoned a stiff drink from Room Service.

THE REST OF THE WORLD XI

Sunil Manohar Gavaskar

(Bombay & India)

BORN:
10 July 1949
Bombay

TEST RECORD:
Bat: 125 matches; 10,122 runs; 236* h.s.; 51.12 average
Bwl: 125 matches; 1 wicket; 1–34 b.b.; 206.00 average

ONE-DAY INT:
Bat: 100 matches; 2,792 runs; 92* h.s.; 34.04 average
Bwl: 100 matches; 1 wicket; 1–10 b.b.; 25.00 average

Gavaskar was scoring hundreds for India before anyone had dreamed up the idea of one-day internationals. In fact he has scored more Test runs than anybody else in the history of the game. It is a myth that he doesn't enjoy instant cricket. Having already proved himself a master technician with phenomenal powers of concentration in Test matches, he now relishes the different challenges posed by the limited-over game.

Don't be misled by his appearance; he's only 5 feet 4 inches but he can hit the ball as hard as anyone. He is strong off his legs in common with most Indian batsmen; a quick flick of the wrists and the ball speeds to the mid-wicket boundary. So we suggest that you encourage your bowlers to concentrate their attack upon off stump. In fact this is the place to bowl at almost any batsman; then it is up to the captain to adjust his fielders according to the batsman's particular strengths and weaknesses.

In the field Gavaskar is quicker than you might expect. He starkly refuses to dive under any circumstances (Indian outfields teach you not to) so he was immediately nicknamed 'Swoop' during his season of county cricket in 1980. An excellent slip fielder. He has a mischievous sense of humour; yet behind that impish grin must lie a hard core of ruthlessness that has given him the will to score so many Test runs.

His Achilles' heel (don't get too excited) is his fear of dogs. I don't see how we can exploit that. It's hard enough for human beings to get past the gatemen at Lord's, let alone canines. And we don't wish to be subjected to the sight of our newly elected captain desperately barking at Gavaskar from first slip.

Geoffrey Robert Marsh

(West Australia & Australia)

BORN:
31 December 1958
Northam, Australia

TEST RECORD:
Bat: 14 matches; 974 runs; 118 h.s.; 38.96 average
Bwl: Has not bowled

ONE-DAY INT:
Bat: 37 matches; 1,179 runs; 125 h.s.; 31.86 average
Bwl: Has not taken any wickets

Marsh's inclusion gives us a contrasting opening pair. Whilst Gavaskar is about to leave the international scene, Marsh has only recently arrived and he seems determined to stay. Their techniques are also different. Whilst Gavaskar is lethal off his legs, Marsh's favourite shots are on the off side – the cover drive and the square cut. He has quickly gained a reputation as a gritty, determined batsman in the Australian tradition of Lawry and Simpson and yet his 1987 World Cup performances showed that he is well suited to the one-day game. As a youngster he used to smash the ball everywhere, but to achieve greater consistency he found it necessary to limit his range of shots.

He has already proven that he enjoys the 'big match atmosphere', which is a handy attribute if you're a Test opener. He says 'the first ball of a Test is often the noisiest of the match. I like that; it really gets the adrenalin flowing.' So he's not going to be terrified by the occasion. He's a good fielder with an excellent pair of hands, probably as a result of chasing and catching sheep down on the farm in Western Australia. Like all good Aussies he'll compete to the bitter end, but after the game he's sure to be more than happy to share a beer with you.

Isaac Vivian Alexander Richards

(Leeward Island & West Indies)

BORN:
7 March 1952
St John's, Antigua

TEST RECORD:
Bat: 88 matches; 6,472 runs; 291 h.s.; 52.61 average
Bwl: 88 matches; 22 wickets; 2–15 b.b.; 54.90 average

ONE-DAY INT:
Bat: 131 matches; 5,196 runs; 189* h.s.; 53.02 average
Bwl: 131 matches; 77 wickets; 5–41 b.b.; 34.40 average

For all our sakes let's hope it's not his day because if it is he can destroy any attack. We still haven't forgotten his innings at Old Trafford in the first Texaco Trophy match of 1984. We had the West Indies reeling at 102–7. Richards proceeded to score a not-out 189 out of a total of 272, the next highest score was 26 by Eldine Baptiste. We could never recover from such a pummelling. He's the finest batsman of this era; however he is not quite so consistent as he was. Sometimes he opts not to play himself in carefully when he first arrives at the crease; instead he attacks from the very first ball. He's vulnerable then, but also very dangerous. Traditionally the hallmark of his play was the whip through mid-wicket played in front of his left pad (not to be found in the *MCC Coaching Manual*), yet recently he has started to score a higher percentage of his runs through the off-side. Despite the above, try not be intimidated by him; after all he is human and he does fail. He will attempt to create a psychological ascendancy even before he takes strike. The way he enters the stage, helmetless and aloof, is designed to undermine his opponents, especially the bowler – a little like a boxer 'winning the weigh-in'.

Of course he's a brilliant fieldsman and, if he bowls, don't underestimate his gentle away-swingers. Overs seem to slip by very quickly when he has the ball. He doesn't waste any time and an uninterrupted Richards over takes about ninety seconds, in contrast to a few of his West Indian colleagues.

Martin David Crowe

(Central Districts & New Zealand)

BORN:
22 September 1962
Auckland

TEST RECORD:
Bat: 36 matches; 2,162 runs; 188 h.s.; 40.79 average
Bwl: 36 matches; 13 wickets; 2–25 b.b.; 46.61 average

ONE-DAY INT:
Bat: 59 matches; 1,640 runs; 105* h.s.; 32.80 average
Bwl: 59 matches; 25 wickets; 2–9 b.b.; 31.24 average

Wags in the crowd, mindful of West Country politics, will probably tell you that your best chance of dismissing nos 3 and 4 is via run-outs. However they are both too professional for that.

It is no longer disputed that Martin Crowe is the finest Kiwi batsman since Martin Donnelly. His upright, clinical style reminded the sages at Taunton of a youthful Greg Chappell – high praise indeed. Like most of the top players, he scarcely allows the bowler a sight of the stumps as the ball is delivered. So there is a chance of trapping him lbw at the start of his innings if he's out of touch. He is also exceptionally strong off his legs so it is imperative that your seamers maintain a tight off-stump line once he has settled in. Against the spinners he is prepared to use his feet to upset their control of length; this means that it is possible to dismiss him stumped. Indeed in domestic cricket in New Zealand left-arm spinner Stephen Boock has had him stumped on numerous occasions – but not before Martin has compiled some formidable scores.

Another fine fieldsman, but a back injury has curtailed his bowling activities. Given the quality of the other bowlers in the side we may regard this as something of a shame.

Allan Robert Border

(Queensland & Australia)

BORN:
27 July 1955
Cremorne, Australia

TEST RECORD:
Bat: 89 matches; 6,917 runs; 196 h.s.; 52.80 average
Bwl: 89 matches; 16 wickets; 3–20 b.b.; 43.68 average

ONE-DAY INT:
Bat: 151 matches; 3,952 runs; 127* h.s.; 32.39 average
Bwl: 151 matches; 23 wickets; 3–21 b.b.; 35.39 average

One of the most tenacious cricketers. He took over the job of captaining Australia because 'there was nobody else'. Since then he has endured heaps of criticism from his own press corps as the national team experienced a lean time. Doggedly he has stuck to his task and helped rebuild a team good enough to win the World Cup final in Calcutta in November 1987. Now he commands respect as a cricketer and a captain wherever he goes in the cricketing world. No one has played in more limited-over internationals than Allan Border; being an Australian has meant that he has had the privilege – or is it the pain? – of playing in all those triangular tournaments down under. He's a mightily effective batsman, rugged rather than stylish. It's a mistake to bowl short to him because the pull and the cut are two of his most productive shots. Against the spinners he, like Crowe, is not frightened to use his feet and in the past he has had some fascinating tussles with Edmonds and Emburey.

Since he was an outstanding baseball player in his youth he possesses a strong arm and a safe pair of hands.

For an Aussie he's pretty shy and retiring, so don't expect too much conversation when you walk out to toss up with him. However as captain he will ensure that the match is played in the right vein. Whatever his alleged shortcomings no one can deny that the atmosphere of the last two Ashes series has been a superb advertisement for cricket. Border should take much of the credit for that.

Imran Khan

(Pakistan)

BORN:
25 November 1952
Lahore

TEST RECORD:
Bat: 70 matches; 2,770 runs; 135* h.s.; 32.97 average
Bwl: 70 matches; 311 wickets; 8–58 b.b.; 22.19 average

ONE-DAY INT:
Bat: 94 matches; 1,638 runs; 102* h.s.; 29.78 average
Bwl: 94 matches; 98 wickets; 6–14 b.b.; 23.56 average

The most accomplished all-rounder ever to come out of Pakistan. The Ladies Stand in Lahore reacts to the presence of Imran Khan in the same way that the teenagers of the sixties responded to Paul McCartney. They squeal a lot. He is good looking, intelligent and immensely gifted. If he was English, he would already be earmarked as a future Chairman of Selectors.

When he left Oxford University in 1975 he was still bowling relatively gentle inswingers; yet within three years he was one of the fastest bowlers in the world, still swinging the ball in – most of the time. Ten years later he has taken a hundred more wickets in Test cricket than any other Pakistani surpassing even Sarfraz Nawaz.

He is a proud man who sets himself, and any Pakistan team which he captains, high standards. Over the years he has worked extremely hard to maintain his fitness and remarkably at the age of thirty-five is still able to keep the best of batsmen loitering on the back foot. He also has the disconcerting knack of swinging the old ball much more than the new one. He has scored well over 2,000 runs in Test cricket, specialising in wristy drives with a slightly inside-out swing of the bat. He is a tentative starter but once he gets the flavour, watch out.

Peter Jeffrey Leroy Dujon
(Jamaica & West Indies)

BORN:
28 May 1956
Kingston, Jamaica

TEST RECORD:
Bat: 43 matches; 2,020 runs; 139 h.s.; 38.11 average
Bwl: has not bowled; 139 catches, 3 stumpings

ONE-DAY INT:
Bat: 100 matches; 1,107 runs; 82* h.s.; 26.35 average
Bwl: has not bowled; 118 catches, 12 stumpings

Dujon has been the West Indies wicket-keeper since 1981. Because he has been such a regular in the team we are hard pushed to name another current West Indian wicket-keeper. The most memorable features of his keeping are those acrobatic diving catches twenty-five yards behind the stumps after someone has edged another thunderbolt from the West Indian pace attack. In fact he has only three stumpings to his name out of 142 Test victims. That's not because he keeps missing them; he never gets any stumping chances. It will be interesting to see him keeping to Abdul Qadir and no doubt he will enjoy this challenge. Certainly he coped with him expertly during the Bicentenary match at Lord's in 1987.

In fact he started his career as a pure batsman (I didn't think you'd be pleased to read that) so beware. He is an effortless timer of the ball and a delight to watch in full flow – unless you are the opposition captain. He's sometimes criticised for being too casual at the crease, needlessly giving his wicket away on occasions. This is maybe because his livelihood doesn't depend exclusively upon how many runs he scores as is the case with specialist batsmen. The other side of the coin is that his keeping gives him a greater freedom to play his shots.

Dujon is a cool customer, who's rarely seen to be agitated on a cricket field, and he's rather good for a no. 7 batsman.

Roger Andrew Harper

(Guyana & West Indies)

BORN:
17 March 1963
Georgetown, Guyana

TEST RECORD:
Bat: 19 matches; 352 runs; 60 h.s.; 16.00 average
Bwl: 19 matches; 40 wickets; 6–57 b.b.; 27.25 average

ONE-DAY INT:
Bat: 48 matches; 286 runs; 45* h.s.; 19.06 average
Bwl: 48 matches; 49 wickets; 3–34 b.b.; 33. 59 average

Anyone seeing Roger Harper for the first time would be surprised – and relieved – to learn that he is an off-spinner rather than another West Indian paceman. He's 6 feet 6 inches tall and on a cricket field looks deadly serious. During the 1987 World Cup he was the West Indies' most effective bowler, spearing down his off-spinners from a height of nine feet or more, whilst occasionally unleashing his 'quicker ball', which bears a greater resemblance to the bowling of Joel Garner than that of Jim Laker. Inevitably he makes the ball bounce more than any of his contemporaries.

He's another dangerous batsman capable of hitting the ball vast distances. He's prepared to hook the faster bowlers and to hit the slower ones 'over the top' – often of the sightscreen.

However, it is in the field where Harper surpasses any other current cricketer. He gobbles up slip catches with the minimum of fuss and in the outfield he is spectacularly brilliant. Like the youthful Clive Lloyd he is capable of swooping on the ball and throwing it all in one movement. He is equally devastating when fielding off his own bowling. Who can forget his run-out of Graham Gooch in the Bicentenary match at Lord's? Having hit a firm straight drive, Gooch was stranded out of his crease, like a rabbit startled and frozen by oncoming headlights. He could just stand and stare as the ball returned like a whiplash, breaking the wickets and leaving him with no alternative but to plod back to the pavilion. Milliseconds earlier he had been thinking in terms of four runs.

Malcolm Denzil Marshall

(Barbados & West Indies)

BORN:
18 April 1958
Pine, Barbados

TEST RECORD:
Bat: 51 matches; 1,068 runs; 92 h.s.; 18.73 average
Bwl: 51 matches; 240 wickets; 7–53 b.b.; 21.64 average

ONE-DAY INT:
Bat: 86 matches; 501 runs; 66 h.s.; 16.70 average
Bwl: 86 matches; 111 wickets; 4–23 b.b.; 22.79 average

Malcolm Marshall is much too good a batsman to be batting at no. 9. For Hampshire he usually comes in at 6 or 7 and that's about right. However you will find that your colleagues will be rather more concerned about his bowling than his batting. For the last three or four years he has become the most feared fast bowler in international cricket. At Headingley in 1984 he bowled England out with his right hand in plaster. During that series there was some media criticism of Marshall's use of the bouncer, however it is interesting to note that there was no condemnation of Marshall from the England players. Gower observed that 'this is a Test match. It's not Old Reptonians versus Lymeswold, one off the mark and jolly good show.' Anyway it is a brave current player, who publicly criticises Marshall.

Be warned that he has two bouncers in his armoury; the first is visible and might possibly be hooked for four. The second is much quicker. However he's not just fast; he's able to bowl outswingers, inswingers and, just occasionally, slower balls; even more impressive, he can quickly assess the strengths and weaknesses of any new opponent and adjust his mode of attack accordingly. I'm afraid he's not even inconsistent or moody like some express bowlers. Whatever the occasion he always gives of his best. And now for the good news – in this match he is entitled to bowl no more than twelve overs.

Abdul Qadir

(Pakistan)

BORN:
15 September 1955
Lahore

TEST RECORD:
Bat: 48 matches; 724 runs; 54 h.s.; 14.19 average
Bwl: 48 matches; 161 wickets; 7–96 b.b.; 34.21 average

ONE-DAY INT:
Bat: 51 matches; 383 runs; 41* h.s.; 16.65 average
Bwl: 51 matches; 74 wickets; 5–44 b.b.; 23.13 average

Abdul Qadir is the best leg-spinner and the most enchanting bowler in the world and he's proved many times that he should not be regarded as a 'luxury' in limited-over cricket. He was one of the most successful bowlers in the recent World Cup; after all it is very difficult for batsmen to premeditate a heave for four if they don't know which way the ball will bounce upon landing and there are not many current international cricketers who can 'pick' Qadir.

He has at his disposal a whole range of different deliveries, but we'll only mention three in case we start to confuse you. They are the leg-spinner (his stock ball, if he can be said to have one), the googly, which looks like a leg-break but is in fact an off-break, and the flipper, which fizzes onto the batsman much quicker than anticipated. In addition he is capable of making the ball dip wickedly at the end of its flight – the sign of a class spinner – so that it is difficult to judge the length of the ball correctly.

He is a bustling, restless, emotional bowler, who likes to attack all the time; indeed he combines the traditional trickery and sleight of hand that we associate with Indian and Pakistani spinners with the outright aggression of an Australian fast bowler. Batsmen may be frightened of being hit by the likes of Malcolm Marshall; they are frightened of being humiliated by Abdul Qadir.

He's also a useful tail-end hitter, who has occasionally saved Pakistan's bacon, for want of a better expression, in the last few decisive overs of a one-day match.

Bruce Anthony Reid

(West Australia & Australia)

BORN:
14 March 1963
Osborne Park, Australia

TEST RECORD:
Bat: 13 matches; 45 runs; 13 h.s.; 5.62 average
Bwl: 13 matches; 41 wickets; 4–64 b.b.; 33.36 average

ONE-DAY INT:
Bat: 33 matches; 35 runs; 10 h.s.; 3.88 average
Bwl: 33 matches; 42 wickets; 5–53 b.b.; 29.90 average

Bruce Reid must be the thinnest, the tallest and maybe the quietest bowler to take the new ball for Australia. When he beats the outside edge of the bat he doesn't bellow his displeasure or his assessment of his opponent down the wicket as we expect Aussie fast bowlers to do. He merely allows himself a wry smile, a knowing glance and then he lopes casually back to his mark. It's all very disconcerting. Mind you, bowling left-arm over the wicket and sliding the ball across the right-handed batsman he beats the bat very frequently, often because of the extra bounce that his height generates.

Reid's rise to international level has been remarkably swift; at the moment he has played more Test matches than state games for his native Western Australia. At the age of twenty-three he found himself spearheading the attack of an unsuccessful Test side; most people would have been satisfied just to have survived this baptism, but Bruce Reid has done a little more than that. Suddenly, after their World Cup victory, Australian confidence is flooding back and, with Craig McDermott back to form, Australia now have a potent, contrasting opening attack, the key to Test success.

He is the obvious choice to bat no. 11 in this side; the gulf between Reid and Qadir is considerable. Bruce is a dependable fieldsman with a reliable pair of hands but despite being the same height as Roger Harper he lacks his agility and explosive pace off the mark. Look for two.

THE UMPIRES

Every good cricket captain tries to keep on the right side of the umpires. You will have two of the best officiating.

DICKIE BIRD

Dickie umpired the first three World Cup finals, but was clearly unable to stand in 1987 because England were finalists and a panel of international umpires had been established for the first time. We cannot understand why he is such a good umpire; he is nervous, fidgety and shy off the field. His colleagues wagered that he would not survive the Indian subcontinent during the 1987 finals either because of illness or hypochondria, but he did. Yet he is universally liked and respected by cricketers all around the globe both as a person and an umpire. His strength as an umpire is simply that he makes very, very few mistakes. You will quickly discover that all those familiar mannerisms are in no way contrived or premeditated to entertain the crowd; they are perfectly natural. When he opens his mouth, you will immediately remember that he hails from Yorkshire.

DAVID SHEPHERD

Compared to Dickie Bird, David Shepherd is a newcomer to the umpires list; he joined after leaving Gloucestershire in 1980. It soon became apparent to all county cricketers that this cuddly Devonian was an excellent umpire, scrupulously fair, yet retaining a keen sense of humour. He was soon appointed to the Test panel and was chosen to accompany Bird to India and Pakistan in 1987. Certainly he would have maintained England's high standing amongst international umpires. We don't know whether he lost any weight, though. He's less flamboyant than his partner, though he does insist upon jumping up and down when the score is on 'Nelson' – 111 or 222 – an old cricketing superstition.

THE MORNING OF THE MATCH

Waking earlier than normal, you go down to the restaurant, collect a plate of bacon and eggs from the counter and sit inconspicuously in a corner of the room. From there you can observe the arrival of some of your new colleagues. First to enter is Phil Edmonds, clutching his *Financial Times*. He has obviously been awake for some time – perhaps he's an insomniac – for he's looking sufficiently alert to have completed a couple of business deals already – perhaps he has.

The same cannot be said for two of the later arrivals, David Gower and Ian Botham. They obviously haven't been awake for a long time. Botham is carrying a copy of the *Sun* and soon he is reading it avidly to find out what he's written about today's match. In between paragraphs he shovels down spoonfuls of the Shredded Wheat, which is quietly overflowing from his cereal bowl; there's scarcely room for three . . . The rest of the side gradually surface; they seem relaxed and happy with one another's company. You notice that there aren't many *Guardian*s about.

You return to your room to slip on your club blazer and tie and to collect your cricket bag. One last look at the mirror just to check that this is really you setting off for Lord's and you're down the lift and walking the two hundred yards to the famous Grace Gates. Already there's hazy sunshine; there will be no rain today. Even the BBC forecasters, so wary and pessimistic since they failed to spot the hurricane of October 1987, are predicting a cloudless day and temperatures rising up into the eighties. Queues of spectators have already formed alongside the new Mound Stand and there are plenty of people milling around by the Grace Gates; fortunately none of them recognises you despite your recent exposure in the national press. Unfortunately neither does the gateman.

'You're captaining England today? Pull the other one.'

You eventually manage to persuade him to ring the offices of the TCCB and the gateman, stunned and crestfallen, allows you in, mumbling about strict instructions from his superior not to . . . You're not interested and you hurry on. Given your experience at the main gate you approach the pavilion in a state of some trepidation. 'I bet Jardine or May or Greig were never refused entry when they led the national team.' A bet you would have won. You are just bracing yourself for another battle with officialdom when you spot that the doorman at the pavilion actually recognises you. He opens the door and wishes you 'Good Morning' very loudly. That's more like it. Your spirits rise; suddenly you're almost starting to feel like an England captain. Almost, but not quite; especially when you realise that you haven't a clue where the Home dressing room is. All credibility rapidly evaporates when you turn and ask the doorman as quietly as possible.

'Where's the dressing room?'

'Sorry, sir. My battery must be flat. I can't hear you.'

You are compelled to ask in a loud voice about the whereabouts of the England dressing room and you can't help noticing one or two members looking over their spectacles at you and then shrugging their shoulders as if to say, 'What's the world coming to?'

Up a short flight of stairs, turn right through the Long Room, two more flights of stairs, right down a corridor of offices, past the physio's room and at the end turn left and you are there.

It's a relief to get to the dressing room, the one sanctuary that a cricketer has on a modern ground. Outside by the door is the notice, 'No one is allowed to enter without the permission of the team manager or captain.' Quite right, too.

Inside you are immediately struck by the spaciousness of the room. In the middle is a huge kitchen table, on which lie the mail and stacks of bats to be signed for worthy county beneficiaries. Along one wall are lockers, which are named; they belong to the Middlesex players; indeed as you arrive Emburey and Downton are both sorting out some kit. Along another are several wash-basins and the third side of this rectangle looks out over the ground itself. The balcony, so tiny in comparison to the rest of the room, is reached simply by opening two rickety glass doors. There are three armchairs and bench seating around the walls.

You introduce yourself to your team and are relieved to find them friendly and welcoming. They help you to feel more at ease; everyone seems remarkably relaxed as if it's just another day at the office. Graham Gooch is making a call on his portable phone, Lamb spends most of his time laughing, Dilley is sorting a few tapes for his Walkman – perhaps he thinks that

England will be batting first, in which case he shouldn't be required until around three o'clock. Bill Athey is meticulously laying out his shirts and flannels, all of which are faultlessly ironed. Botham arrives at 9.48, three minutes late; you decide not to make an issue of it. He playfully moves Foster's kit to one side declaring that he's 'changed here for the last dozen years' and then asks the dressing room attendant to pop some tickets on the gate since 'the whole lot are coming today'. Gradually between conversations everyone arranges their kit from their massive coffins and they get changed and slowly the conversations focus upon the day's game. You quickly realise that the light-hearted atmosphere of the dressing room does not reflect a 'couldn't care less attitude'; it's just that the players know that there are going to be plenty of pressure points throughout the day and it's better to avoid being too earnest and tense an hour before the game starts. There'll be plenty of time for that later on.

The players now set out for the Nursery to stretch, bowl a few balls in the nets or feel the bat on the ball. On the way over you stop to examine the wicket since you need to be clear in your mind what you'll do if you win the toss. You find that there is not much grass on the wicket but there are signs that it still retains a little moisture. Spotting that Allan Border has just had a brief conversation with the groundsman you follow suit. He informs you that it may seam a little early on but within an hour it will dry out into a 'belter'; any turn will be slow. Chatting to some of your colleagues you discover that most of the batsmen want to bat first, whilst the bowlers want to bowl first. It's your decision. Ponder it over a cup of tea in the dressing room.

At 10.25 you borrow an England blazer, find a ten-pence piece and walk the forty yards along the corridor to the opposition dressing room. Swallowing hard you knock on the door with as much authority as you can muster: you open the door and ask for the captain. Allan Border sees you, grabs his much-travelled green blazer and comes over to shake your hand. Down the stairs, through a curious Long Room and you stride out towards the square. The ground is almost full now and interest is awakened by the emergence of the captains, the first piece of drama in the day. Allan Border is clearly enjoying the atmosphere.

'Nothing beats Lord's on a day like this. I've played in front of

90,000 at Melbourne and Calcutta, but Lord's is special.'

You agree without bothering to mention that you haven't yet experienced a capacity crowd at Calcutta. It is undoubtedly a handsome sight but you are still a little preoccupied. Bat or bowl? Bat or bowl?

On the square Border gives the wicket a ritual prod; he's not looking for any clues; he has the air of a man who has made his mind up. Loitering nearby is the groundsman, still fretting over his wicket as if it were a new-born child, and the umpires who are about to 'receive' the wicket from the groundsman. Border greets them like old friends, briefly reminding David Shepherd of his few appearances for Gloucestershire 2nd XI in the 1970s. The umpires both shake your hand politely after Border has made the introductions. Somehow the whole process reminds you of your inexperience, even though Border is doing his best to put you at your ease. Bat or bowl?

'Right, we'd better get on with it. My team is Gavaskar, Marsh and Richards, Martin Crowe at four, myself, Imran, Dujon, Harper, Marshall at nine, Abdul and Bruce Reid.'

You realise that teams have to be exchanged.

'Gooch, Athey, Gower, Lamb, myself (here you are desperately trying to maintain a matter-of-fact tone), Botham, Downton, Emburey, Foster, Edmonds and Dilley.'

Out of courtesy you demonstrate that your ten-pence coin possesses both a head and a tail and you flick it high into the sky. Bat or bowl? Bat or bowl? Border says:

'I'll have a head, thanks.'

The coin lands some five yards away from where you're standing. You move towards it, hopefully without indecent haste. Together you bend down to see a head staring innocently up at you. Is there just a flicker of relief?

'You have a hit.'

Obviously that's the Australian for 'I have decided that my team will field first.' Border shakes your hand and returns the coin.

'Good luck, have a good game, mate.' As you set off back to the pavilion you can't help feeling that this Australian is really far more civilised than you had been led to believe. He had gone out of his way to make you feel comfortable and you felt that a bond, no matter how small, had been established between the two captains. Perhaps the day wouldn't be quite as difficult as you imagined.

Back in the dressing room your players are anxious to know the outcome. Once you've informed them you take the opportunity to wish everyone the best of luck, however you decide not to deliver an oration of Churchillian dimensions, just a few well chosen words of encouragement. Meanwhile Gooch and Athey are calmly going through their trusted routine, arranging their batting gear and playing a few imaginary shots. Gooch shows the twelfth man, a youngster on the Lord's ground staff, his favourite floppy hat, which is to be brought out once the spinners come on. You are impressed by such confidence. The attendant asks who wants lunch in the dressing room; more telegrams arrive. Dilley, now able to relax for a while, puts on his Walkman. Edmonds makes a phone call. Gower, with the casual brilliance of his batting, glances at Paul Downton's crossword and answers a clue. Lamb, impressed, comes over to try to do the same. After thirty seconds he loses patience, declares that crosswords are a waste of time and yells across the room, asking if 'Beefy' (Botham) has finished with the *Sun*. As captain you are now virtually powerless to influence events until it is your turn to bat.

The bell rings. Foster, on the balcony shouts, 'They're out there,' and amidst a chorus of 'Good lucks' Gooch and Athey leave the dressing room. Fifty seconds later generous applause greets them as they enter cricket's noblest stage.

ENGLAND BATTING

Up in the Warner Stand the familiar signature tune faded and the lilting tones of Tony Lewis welcomed BBC viewers to Lord's for this unique match. Next door in the press box a good proportion of the cricket journalists had made it for the start. Beneath Old Father Time in the scoreboard the scorers had by now sharpened their pencils and established who was hiding under the various floppy hats on view. The groundstaff enjoyed a few moments of well deserved relaxation down by the covers at the Nursery End. Even the Mound Stand, one of the havens for the sponsors' guests, was full before the first ball was bowled. In Q stand the players' wives and guests greeted each other fulsomely whilst silently monitoring new hairstyles. In the hallowed pavilion itself, the Committee Room bar steward poured the first gin and tonic of the day; it would not be the last.

Inside the England dressing room, Gower, your no. 3, is now ready; he is standing just inside the balcony, from where he'll have a good view of the opening over. He wants to check the pace and bounce of the wicket and look for signs of swing. Lamb has his thigh pad and box in position so that he could be ready to face the hat-trick ball without being timed out, heaven forbid. You move out on to the balcony, cricket's equivalent of the captain being on the bridge and Marshall hurtling in from the pavilion end bowls to Gooch. The ball passes harmlessly into the gloves of Dujon.

Gooch, with a firm push past mid-on's left hand, opens the scoring off the last ball of the over. Against Imran, Athey gets off the mark with a deflection to long leg. Like the opening round of a heavyweight contest, both sides opt to begin cagily. Neither Marshall nor Imran strives for optimum pace initially, whilst Athey and even Gooch are content to try to pick up singles. After all, sixty overs is a long time.

Up on the balcony you observe not only the cricket but also your colleagues. They all know precisely what's happening out in the middle, yet at the same time most of them appear preoccupied with something else. Downton is now whitening his wicket-keeping pads, Emburey is signing the bats on the table, Foster is putting another grip on his bat, a sure sign that he takes his batting seriously; he has three bats in his coffin to Dilley's one. Edmonds is still on the phone. Yet, when Gooch straight drives Marshall for the first boundary of the innings, everyone acknowledges the shot and urges him – ridiculously – to keep going. Gooch can't hear the wise words of the dressing room, but that won't stop a steady stream of advice throughout the day.

After eight overs the score is 19-0 and Border opts to replace Marshall with Reid. This represents a minor triumph for your opening batsmen since Marshall's first spell has been wicket-less, an unusual occurrence. Athey and Gooch, who is beginning to look a little more belligerent, step up the tempo. Athey cuts the first ball of Reid's third over to the square-cover boundary, his first four. Even Sir Geoffrey would have been proud of that one – 38-0. However the next ball is quicker and jags back down the slope and raps Athey on the left pad. There's a loud appeal; the dressing room falls silent awaiting Dickie Bird's decision; they know it's close, but Dickie likes to give the batsman the benefit of any doubt. He raises his finger and Athey sets off for the pavilion, whilst Reid is congratulated by his team-mates.

In the pavilion Gower slips on his blue helmet, mumbles to no one in particular 'My turn, then' and quietly leaves the room. Athey returns and is given ten minutes breathing space by his colleagues. Batsmen all have different routines after dismissal; some rant and rave, others mumble to themselves with a mixture of disbelief and self-recrimination, whilst there's a small minority who casually continue reading the paper that they'd started before their innings as if nothing had happened at all. It depends too on the mode of dismissal. If they have been dismissed by an 'unplayable ball' that pitches leg and hits off, then most players accept this as a 'good dismissal'; but if they've played a poor shot or been the victim of a dubious umpiring decision, the sparks tend to fly.

In this case Athey recovers quickly and tells Lamb, who has now popped his pads on, that it's a typical easy-paced Lord's wicket.

'Once it's dried out completely it'll be a beaut,' he adds ruefully.

Now you slip on your box and thigh pad and you notice that your palms are a little damp. Your time is drawing nearer. But like any good captain you are of course more concerned about your team's progress than your individual fate.

There doesn't seem to be too much to worry about as Gower starts to play exquisitely, clipping Abdul Qadir who has replaced Imran at the Nursery End wide of mid-on for four and then square-cutting him up the hill for another. Border is forced to replace Qadir with the off spin of Roger Harper and all is well with the world. Up in the Radio 3 commentary box 'Johnners' is welcoming World Service listeners one moment, thanking Mrs Gullidge of Littlehampton for her chocolate cake the next and then purring with delight at another Gower cover drive before handing over to Trevor Bailey for a more clinical assessment of what is going on. Listeners are informed that Gooch and Gower are 'playing very sensibly' and that they are both 'very fine players indeed'.

The dressing room grows gradually noisier as the partnership progresses; several of the players go out on to the balcony rather than watching the TV on top of the lockers. They look out for their friends in Q stand and begin to enjoy the occasion. The fall of a wicket would of course transform the atmosphere but all seems secure. Allan Lamb, the next man in, fidgets, nervously chewing gum; all the while he's chattering away to nobody in particular. Sometimes he makes sense; at others the thread is lost, never to be recovered, after a narrow squeak out in the middle. In the 28th over Gooch drives Harper easily to long-on to register his fifty. The crowd applauds and you make a point of being on the balcony yourself as he reaches this landmark.

The tension increases as Border switches around his bowlers just before lunch. No one wants to bat for ten minutes before the interval and it would be marvellous to go into lunch with nine wickets standing. The last over is bowled by Marshall and Border puts in a second slip as he senses that the batsmen are now intent upon survival. Marshall is still capable of hurrying the batsmen even though they are well set. Gooch picks up a streaky single to long leg. Gower plays and misses and looks totally unconcerned; he ducks a bouncer and sets off for some lunch. Gooch, as if emphasising his intention to occupy the crease for a while yet, leaves his gloves and helmet on the wicket to dry in the midday sun. A lone bobby comes out to guard them. The Long Room stands to applaud the players of both sides and the bars around the ground fill up. The score is 110-1 after 33 overs.

Before going upstairs for lunch, you await the return of your two batsmen. On their arrival you congratulate them and they quietly acknowledge your remarks. However neither is looking too pleased with himself since they both recognise that their job is only half finished.

They now have half an hour in which to relax and recharge their batteries. Unhurriedly they remove their pads, drink some squash and settle down for some lunch on the kitchen table; the dressing room attendant bustles around catering for their needs – more squash, some ice cream, a pot of tea. They watch the afternoon news on the television, read the paper. Gooch decides on a quick shower; Gower finishes Paul Downton's crossword and thinks about doing Allan Lamb's for him.

Upstairs in the cosy players' dining room Nancy has produced one of her delicious roasts; not only does it taste good, but it's served swiftly so everyone is happy. Over the years Nancy has won the hearts of all professional cricketers through her cooking and her no-nonsense sense of humour. She personally delivers Botham, an old friend since his Lord's ground-staff days, a plate stacked with five thick slices of roast beef. Amidst the jeers Ian points out – a little defensively – that he no longer eats potatoes. It is no wonder that some Middlesex players have a tendency towards portliness. Within twenty-five minutes the players are back in the dressing room; there's plenty of noise, an indication that spirits are high. The morning session has given the side an excellent platform from which to attack in the afternoon and the players see the possibility of a score in excess of 250. John Emburey, maybe sensing some complacency, reminds everyone that 'there's a long way to go in our innings yet'. Twenty-seven overs, to be precise. The bell clangs and Gooch and Gower set off. Allan Lamb puts his pads back on, whilst you resume your position on the balcony; after all, things had gone pretty well when you were sitting there in the morning and whilst you're not superstitious . . .

The crowd is anxious for play to restart, except perhaps for the sponsors' guests who are still supping in the massive marquee alongside the indoor school. However through a haze of cigar smoke the real enthusiasts can watch proceedings on the large television screens placed in the corners of the marquee.

Border chooses to start with Abdul Qadir from the Nursery

End. Gooch checks his guard and Umpire Shepherd calls 'Play'. Qadir flicks the ball mesmerically from hand to hand, walks two paces, trots three and then fizzes the ball down the wicket. A second later Richie Benaud up in the BBC commentary box is in ecstasy.

'Bowled him. My word, what a wonderful piece of wrist-spin bowling that was from Abdul Qadir.'

Benaud, a former leg-spinner himself, laments the demise of the modern leg-spinner and enjoys watching Qadir more than any other bowler. It reminds him of his youth.

Qadir had opted to bowl his flipper the first ball after lunch. Gooch sensing that the ball was short went back to cut. It hurried on quicker than he expected. A faint inside edge and the ball skidded into the off stump. Gooch looks to the skies and plods off towards the pavilion. Allan Lamb takes a deep breath, checks that he's wearing his box and leaves the dressing room. You move in from the balcony and start to buckle up your pads. Your time is drawing near.

Out in the middle Lamb takes guard and surveys the field. Qadir, who was so delighted to grab the prized wicket of Gooch, loses concentration briefly and bowls a no-ball which Lamb clips to deep backward square leg for a single, a confident start. The next ball is slightly overpitched and Gower straight-drives with surprising power. Qadir dives to his right and his finger-tips just touch the ball, which ricochets on to the stumps at the bowler's end. Inside the pavilion you hear the loud appeal as you are doing up the last buckle. You look up just in time to see David Shepherd's raised index finger. You're in. You are vaguely aware of the groans of your team-mates, something along the lines of 'what rotten luck' as you nervously put on your gloves; then as you leave the comfort of the dressing room there are shouts of encouragement. The score is 111-3. Nelson has struck. And you're in.

BATTING

You walk down the stairs. There are still some members yet to return to their seats after lunch; you have to sidestep one or two, who appear completely oblivious to your inner turmoil. In the Long Room those on the high chairs swing around curiously as you pass Allan Lamb. There is polite applause, though you cannot tell whether this is directed sympathetically at Lamb or as a mild encouragement to you. Out the door, down the steps and through the gate, which has been opened by another steward and a capacity Lord's Cricket Ground awaits you. Up in the Radio 3 commentary box Christopher Martin-Jenkins describes your entry to his listeners and then turns hopefully to Bill Frindall, the 'Bearded Wonder', for some sort of statistical record of your career. The only record that emerges is that this is the first time at a Lord's showpiece that Frindall has been reduced to silent impotence. He has no statistics. No one knows what to expect.

Gower recognising that you might be a touch nervous comes out to greet you and he warns you to watch out for Qadir's flipper early on. Umpire Shepherd gives you your guard.

'Right arm over the wicket; four balls to come.'

Border has already posted Gavaskar at slip and now he chooses to delay Qadir and to position himself four feet from the bat at silly point. You smile uneasily at him. At least, a familiar face. Border's eyes stare piercingly at you, through you. He seemed such a nice chap when you tossed up together three hours ago; now you sense nothing but hostility. He claps his hands and shouts encouragement at Qadir, who is licking his fingers, eager, impatient, sensing an opportunity. The crowd is hushed. Qadir bowls. Mindful of Gower's advice you push forward. Sure enough, the ball hurries on much more quickly than you expect and you are rapped on the pad. Qadir, Dujon, even Border, appeal confidently. After a moment's contemplation – it seems an age – Shepherd responds firmly, 'That's not out.'

The next ball is tossed higher into the air. It looks like a half-volley, but at the end of its flight it dips, drops and spins past the outside edge of your bat. Qadir looks down the wicket at you, frowning at the injustice of it all. Gower tries an encouraging smile. You pat down an imaginary blemish in the pitch, just to try to allay your nerves. Border decides to add to your feeling of claustrophobia by bringing Geoff Marsh in to forward short leg. He doesn't even bother to put a helmet on. Suddenly you think of Mike Denness. He must have felt just like this when captaining England on the ill-fated 1974/5 tour of Australia. Lillee and Thomson were in full flight and England's captain was short of confidence. This wasn't helped by the fact that, every time he arrived at the wicket, he could overhear Doug Walters moaning in the gully: 'Oh no; we're going to be held up for at least another ten minutes now.'

Strangely this thought cheers you up a little.

The fifth ball of the over is well flighted, pitching on middle stump. You play a forward defensive stroke and contact! At least you've hit one, though as yet you can't imagine how you are going to get the scoreboard moving. The ball trickles towards extra cover; no run. You notice that Qadir runs up to the wicket a little wider of the crease for the last delivery of the over. The ball is tossed higher than the previous three and it is wide of the off stump. It appears to be full in length. Do you

A. attempt a full-blooded cover drive. Or

B. settle for a forward defensive shot.

If **A** turn to page 50
If **B** turn to page 52

A. Again the ball dips at the end of its flight as you attempt the cover drive. As a result you are not quite at the pitch of the ball. Even worse you discover – too late – that this is Qadir's googly. The inside edge of the bat makes contact with the ball, which spoons gently, pathetically to the mid-wicket fieldsman, Harper, who completes one of the easiest catches of his career. The crowd groans, Qadir and Border are jubilant. Richie Benaud, on air, explains that 'Qadir simply knew too much for him'. Bill Frindall jots down your career record and files it away, wondering whether he'll ever have to refer to it again.

Studying your toecaps you return to the pavilion. In the Long Room a deathly silence greets you and it's not much different when you get back to the dressing room. There are a few 'bad lucks' but deep down you know it wasn't bad luck. You had been completely outwitted. If only you could face that ball again. A restless night and two hours glued to the seat on the balcony, anxiously contemplating your innings, and it's all over in four balls. What a waste: of time; of mental energy; and what a wasted opportunity. Your head sinks between your knees. You feel desperate. The Chairman of Selectors is none too thrilled either as he begins to speculate upon the headlines of Sunday morning's sports' pages. The attendant brings over a glass of squash, out of habit more than anything. You can't really be thirsty; you've only been gone ten minutes, yet you drink it out of politeness. Twenty minutes ago the dressing room was buoyant and the score was 110-1; now there's a tense silence and the score is 111-4.

Whilst you are in despair, outside the crowd have already forgotten about the England captain's demise. Botham's in and they have moved to the edge of their seats. When confronted by a crisis – and losing three wickets for one run constitutes a crisis – Botham reacts predictably. Like a cornered lion he lashes out fiercely. He edges Qadir for four to third man; he mishooks Marshall for a single down to long leg and in the next over smashes Qadir over extra cover for four. Gower, meanwhile, continues to play serenely and more conservatively than Botham (which is not difficult) as if to say 'Crisis? What crisis?'

At the end of the 43rd over he sweeps Harper for a single to take him to fifty and the total to 150-4. Back in the dressing room you are feeling slightly less suicidal now. You may have failed with the bat, but you still have the chance to lead England to victory. Brearley didn't score hundreds and fifties that often for England and yet he was a vital member of the side. It is important that you put to one side any personal disappointment. Soon you're on the balcony, cheering misfields, calling runs, setting targets. The batsmen still can't hear you, but that doesn't seem to matter.

In the middle Botham is blazing away and thoroughly enjoying himself, as are the 25,000 spectators. You make a point of registering the Chairman's reaction when he reverse-sweeps Harper to the boundary. However, in the off-spinner's final over Botham is effortlessly caught by Marshall at long on, making the score 193-5 from 51 overs, Botham 45. On his return you are intrigued that Botham doesn't chide himself for hitting the ball in the air, rather for not going through with the shot.

'I didn't really hit it. I stopped my shot just at the end. It should have ended up on our balcony.' He's annoyed, but doesn't sulk. He didn't get where he is today by sulking.

Downton ensures that Gower has most of the strike now. Gower responds by hitting two silky fours but Imran gets his revenge, having him caught behind flashing outside the off stump. However, not even his sternest critics could complain about this shot or this innings, a magnificent 92. The members give him a standing ovation. Gower acknowledges their applause by removing his helmet and permitting himself a sheepish grin. 227-6 after 55 overs.

The last five overs of the innings produce another 37 runs. Emburey, with no backlift and looking tentative, to say the least, against the fast bowlers still contrives to hit three boundaries, one a remarkable sliced six into the Tavern. Downton scurries between the wickets. Marshall claims two well deserved victims and off the last ball of the innings Edmonds is run out, whilst still trying to maintain his dignity. The final score is 264-9 and Dilley is relieved not to have to bat.

It could have been a lot worse.

Turn to page 96

B. This is Qadir's googly and with a mixture of bat and pad your forward defensive shot smothers the ball. You survive. It's the end of the over and since you're feeling a little exposed you're pleased to see Gower coming down the pitch for a chat.

'Well played, David.' This is the sort of thing that you imagine a captain should say to his batsmen. 'What's happening out here?'

'Abdul's getting a bit of turn. Watch out for that quicker one and his googly. You spotted that last one well.' You wonder whether to tell him the truth. 'Malcolm's coming on this end. Good luck.'

Gower on 34 clips the first ball of Marshall's over down to long leg for a single. You take guard and look around the field. Border has stationed two slips for an outside edge. As you focus upon Marshall, you are surprised by the size of him; there's nothing to him; he's only 5 feet 9 inches at the most. Can he really be that quick?

Marshall sprints up to the wicket and into his bowling action. The next thing you know the ball is whistling past your nose as you rock backwards taking instinctive evasive action. You just manage to avoid toppling over completely as the ball thuds into Dujon's gloves, which are held above his head. Marshall stares down the wicket unsmilingly and for a second you think that you spot the tiniest of grins on Gower's face. Two thoughts enter your head – 'That was quick' and 'That nearly knocked my head off'. Marshall asks Border for an extra close catcher at forward short leg and Marsh is brought in from mid-wicket. Again no helmet. The last ball you received was quicker than anything you'd ever seen before; hopefully it was his 'quicker' bouncer. As you settle into your stance you have a decision to make. Do you

A. consciously move your foot back and across, in anticipation of another short-pitched delivery, so that you have more time to see the ball? Or

B. stand as you normally do and look to get forward?

If **A** turn to page 54
If **B** turn to page 56

Abdul Qadir – a formidable proposition on arrival at the crease

A. Back and across you go. However, to your surprise Marshall pitches the ball right up – an attempted yorker. You are still on the back foot when the ball just kisses the inside edge of your bat, before thundering into your right ankle. The pain is excruciating; somehow the ball has avoided all your padding; you let out an involuntary yell and wince; the world seems to be rotating rather quicker than it should.

The next thing you're aware of is David Gower advancing towards you, looking more animated than normal, shouting 'Run, run'. Even though you have absolutely no idea of the whereabouts of the ball, you're just grateful to be able to obey a command and, forgetting the pain, you hurtle down to the non-striker's end as best you can. By now Richards is attending the stumps and, upon hearing him shout 'This end', you sense danger especially when you see him cup hands in preparation for catching the ball. You decide to dive. It is not an elegant dive, but effective. You've made it and start to sigh with relief; then you spot Richards giggling as the ball is gently returned to Dujon by Crowe. Richards had been bluffing; there had never been any danger. Once you started running Crowe at square leg had conceded the single. As you dust yourself off Gower comes down the wicket:

'We must keep on the look-out for singles. That was an easy one. Anyway, well done; you're off the mark.'

Amidst the mayhem you had completely overlooked this landmark and the pain in your ankle seems to recede a little. The next ball is a bouncer and you're amazed how easily and gracefully Gower sways out of the way. He has so much time. The final ball of the over is of full length and Gower stands up and drives it through extra cover for four.

116-3 from 35 overs. You are now facing the first ball of Qadir's next over. It is a little short of a length just outside the off stump. Bearing in mind how well you're seeing the ball do you

A. play a full-blooded cut shot? Or
B. play defensively?

If **A** turn to page 73
If **B** turn to page 58

Malcolm Marshall – the quickest bowler you've ever faced

B. Having decided that it's too late for any major technical overhauls, you stand normally, determined simply to watch the ball and to play straight. Marshall bowls a full-length ball on middle and leg stump. Without thinking you react, making good contact with the ball which goes into the vacant mid-wicket area. The famous Lord's slope maintains its momentum and two runs result. You are off the mark and immediately feel more confident.

The next ball from Marshall is shorter. You get up on your toes and play it down defensively to forward short leg. You feel a sense of relief. True, Marshall is quicker than anything you've experienced before but you can see the ball. It is less terrifying in the middle than watching on the balcony. The final ball of the over is a little short outside the off stump and you cut it past cover point's left hand. Qadir at third man has a long run around the boundary and you have time to scamper three more runs. Dickie Bird bellows 'Over' and Gower moves down the wicket towards you.

'Well played, skip. Everything OK?'

You reply that it is and it dawns upon you that you are really enjoying yourself. You know that during that last over you have impressed your partner and proved you're not a joker and, once you have won the confidence of your team-mates, anything is possible. You are as alert and alive as you've ever been. The adrenalin is pumping around your veins like a river in full spate. Gower is a little calmer and as you separate suggests that 'you keep playing sensibly and positively'. 116-3 from 35 overs. You are now facing the first ball of Qadir's next over. It is a little short of a length pitching just outside the off stump. Bearing in mind how well you're seeing the ball do you

A. play a full-blooded square cut? Or

B. play defensively?

If **A** turn to page 73
If **B** turn to page 58

At the other end, David Gower's batting remains serene and effortless

B. The ball rolls harmlessly to Harper at cover point. No run. Qadir looks relieved. You are still feeling tentative against Qadir's wrist spin and you are indebted to Gower's alertness for getting you away from the strike. Twice your defensive prod has resulted in the ball trickling behind square on the on side from an inside edge. Both times he's called you for singles so that Border decides to move his cover point to square leg.

Over the next four overs the tempo of the game changes. Gower is able to manipulate singles at will, though boundaries are proving elusive. However, you are finding it difficult to keep the scoreboard ticking over. In the commentary box Henry Blofeld feels compelled to enliven proceedings by relating the movements of a pigeon at deep extra cover. In the press box the flurry that followed two quick wickets subsides and one innocent, new to the job, offers to buy a drink. Bar trade improves in the committee rooms, as well. However, in the English dressing room your colleagues watch with renewed interest and concern – except Phil Edmonds who is on the phone.

To an outsider this passage of play simply looks like a 'quiet period'. In fact it represents something of a crisis. England have to regain the initiative soon and you are beginning to feel the pressure. Gower attempts to keep you relaxed, telling you 'not to worry; the singles will come; keep on the look-out for them'. But four overs slip by for just ten runs, seven of which are scored by Gower, taking the score to 126-3 from 39 overs and you have been monopolising the strike.

You clip the first ball of Qadir's over firmly off your legs to the left of Dickie Bird and immediately take a couple of strides down the wicket. Gower dutifully awaits your call. Do you yell
A. 'Yes'? Or
B. 'No'?

If **A** turn to page 60
If **B** turn to page 62

Abdul Qadir sizes up his new adversary

A. Gower responds as best he can but the odds are always against him. If only you had remembered that Harper had been moved to square leg; if Gavaskar or Reid had been fielding there a single would have been a formality. As it is there is only just enough time for the batsmen to cross before Dujon removes the bails after Harper's immaculate pick-up and throw. Gower doesn't bother looking at the umpire, but just keeps on running towards the pavilion, where he receives sympathetic applause. There's a pause whilst the crowd awaits the emergence of Botham, long enough for you to mull over your mistake. In your desperation to get away from the strike you had panicked and forgotten about the field placements.

Botham strides out of the pavilion swinging his mighty bat through 360 degrees to stretch his muscles. At least you know that he relishes a crisis and losing three wickets for just 16 runs just about constitutes a crisis. Before taking guard he comes down the wicket to you.

'Forget about what's gone before. Oh, and I'll do the calling for a while. OK?'

Botham plays his first ball defensively to Harper at square leg and bellows 'No' at full volume. He can't resist a smile. He drives his third ball over extra cover for four and doesn't bother to run – or call. He doesn't appear to be inhibited by the situation. Indeed the next three overs see an improvement in England's position. Thanks mostly to Botham's controlled aggression 19 runs are scored. Marshall is withdrawn from the attack and replaced by Harper and a vicious Botham straight drive forces Qadir to leave the field for repairs.

For the first time since lunch the Rest of the World are under pressure; they are temporarily a bowler short; the score has risen to 151-4 from 43 overs and following Botham's forthright example you have managed your first boundary, an authentic cover drive off Harper.

Please turn to page 63

A disconsolate Gower makes for the pavilion steps

B. Just in time you shout 'No' as you recall that Roger Harper has recently been moved to square leg. Even so you have to scramble to get back, diving desperately and becoming entangled with Dujon, who seems to find the whole episode remarkably amusing. He's seen Harper cause chaos many times before. Gower calls out from the other end: 'Good decision.'

Another outside edge gives Gower the strike. He lofts the next ball over the infield, bisecting deep mid-wicket and long-on perfectly. Clearly he has decided to up the tempo. However, when he tries to repeat the shot, the ball goes squarer than planned and Crowe on the boundary takes a fine running catch. 131-4. Gower receives warm applause from the members in the pavilion and Botham strides out swinging his massive Duncan Fearnley in an arc of 360 degrees; this is to loosen up his muscles as well as being a declaration of intent. Bars around the ground empty and there's an air of expectancy, though, with Botham at the crease, no one knows precisely what to expect.

He smashes his third ball from Qadir over extra cover for four, a characteristic method of getting off the mark and the run-rate improves. Marshall bowls one more over and is then replaced by Harper; obviously Border wants to save a few Marshall overs for 'the death'. A vicious Botham straight drive is painfully stopped by Qadir forcing him to leave the field for repairs and for the first time since lunch the Rest of the World are under pressure; they are temporarily a bowler short; the score has risen to 151-4 from 43 overs and following Botham's forthright example you have managed your first boundary, an authentic cover-drive off Harper.

Please turn to page 63

Now Border decides to gamble. With Qadir still off the field, he has to find an over from a non-specialist bowler and surprisingly he chooses himself. In the World Cup he had proved to be a most effective sixth bowler, often breaking up dangerous partnerships, with his unassuming left-arm spinners. In addition he's been a close friend of Botham as well as being a team-mate in the Queensland side during the 1987/8 Australian season. He reasons that Botham will react in one of two ways; either he will play with uncharacteristic caution, since he won't want to suffer the indignity of being humiliated by one of his mates, who happens to be a part-time bowler into the bargain; or, the challenge will be irresistible for Botham, who will try to hit every ball out of the ground, with the likelihood that he'll sacrifice his wicket in the process, thereby opening up the England tail for his recognised bowlers. It is undoubtedly a brave move and, as Border goes about setting his field, you mull over its implications. Should you have a word with Botham, giving him your analysis of Border's motives? You decide to keep quiet for the moment; after all, during the last few overs the situation has improved. Why complicate matters?

Botham is clearly surprised by the change of bowling and, suppressing a wry grin, he settles into his stance. Border trots up and bowls and to your horror Botham plays a reverse sweep shot; not even a good reverse sweep shot. Didn't he watch the World Cup final? The ball lobs up into the air towards the vacant first slip area. Dujon back-pedals and dives full-stretch; the ball just eludes him and Border squeals with anguish. As Dujon dusts himself off you move down the wicket for a chat with your all-rounder. Do you

A. instruct him firmly not to play the reverse sweep at this stage of his innings since it is clearly jeopardising your recovery? Or

B. humour him by suggesting playfully that he should play the reverse sweep to every single ball?

If **A** turn to page 64
If **B** turn to page 66

A. Your instruction is greeted with a stony silence, which hides, not very convincingly, a mixture of disbelief and anger. You wonder about the wisdom of your remark; equally you are pretty intrigued how Botham will combat Border's next delivery. He returns to his crease; there's no hint of a smile now. As Border turns he is pounding his bat into the hallowed turf. At the moment of delivery he advances down the wicket, opens his shoulders and straight drives the ball on to the top of the hospitality marquee, waking a keen tennis player, who had one port too many at lunchtime. Botham stares down the wicket at you and shouts: 'Happy now?'

You find it difficult to assess what is the correct response to this question and opt for an uneasy silence. Botham reverse-sweeps the third ball of Border's over to the third-man boundary; still no smile. The fourth lands on top of the marquee and our tennis player dives under the table presuming that he's under enemy attack. Botham blocks the fifth ball, with exaggerated care, and now a broad smile beams down the wicket though you are not sure whether it's directed at you or Allan Border. For good measure he reverse-sweeps the final ball of the over for a single, thereby keeping the strike.

The mid-wicket conference that follows this over can only be described as 'interesting'. The cameras zoom in and television viewers attempt to lip-read; you decide to keep the content of the conversation to yourself. Perhaps you may divulge it to your grandchildren in a few years, by which time you'll be doing more of the talking.

Four runs come from Harper's next over, leaving you on strike. 172-4 from 45 overs. Border decides not to risk another over and turns to Vivian Richards to fill in Abdul's missing quota; he has two to bowl and you must decide whether

A. to join Botham in all out assault on Richards? Or

B. to be content with a supporting role and to play more carefully?

If **A** turn to page 67
If **B** turn to page 69

Botham asks: 'Who is this man at the other end?'

B. Sure enough Botham carefully reverse-sweeps the next ball for a single and guffaws as he trots down the wicket. Up on the balcony the Chairman shakes his head and on BBC TV Ray Illingworth sensibly wonders about the percentages of such a shot. In the middle you wonder about the effectiveness of your psychology.

Having played two balls firmly but straight to the fielders you rush down the wicket to Border and swing fiercely. The ball spoons over extra cover and just trickles down the slope over the ropes. You try to repeat the shot to the next ball, which is a little wider. You miss completely and scramble desperately back to your crease. Dujon takes the bails off and appeals.

'Not Out', but it must have been very close. There now follows the unlikely sight of Botham coming down the wicket to urge caution telling you that this is not a friendly Saturday afternoon thrash amongst friends. It's vital for the side that you regain concentration. Just because Border is not a recognised bowler it doesn't mean that he's not dangerous. 155-4 from 44 overs.

You recognise the truth of all this and try to collect your thoughts and recover your concentration. It's all very well sharing a joke with Botham but, if it affects the way you play, then it's time to call a halt. You are here to win the match, not to be part of a comedy duo. However, as you're contemplating all these matters there's an uproar from the direction of the Tavern. Looking up you catch sight of a female streaker jumping over the fence and then galloping towards the middle at full speed. She seems to be heading for Botham. This is all you need as you're trying to get in the right frame of mind for the next over.

A. Do you steadfastly ignore this intrusion, fearing that it might upset your concentration further? Or

B. Do you give her your fullest attention and enjoy the fun?

If **A** turn to page 68
If **B** turn to page 70

A. You opt for the aggressive approach. After all, any bowler, no matter how accomplished, is at his most tentative at the start of his spell. Also, although there are now sixteen overs left a fair proportion of those will be bowled by Marshall, Imran and Reid and they are pretty tricky to smash around the ground. You can't leave everything to Botham.

You square-cut the first ball crisply to the boundary. Botham nods his approval from the other end. Off the next a leg glance brings two runs and from the final ball of the over you play a lofted off-drive which just eludes the outstretched arms of Reid at mid-off. Ten from the over and Border's team is on the defensive. Trevor Bailey notes that the captain is playing with 'immense commonsense'; indeed your last shot is deemed to be good enough to warrant four action-replays on the TV. Border now decides to try to halt this run-glut by bringing back Imran Khan from the Pavilion End. He positions five men on the leg side, suggesting that he is going to direct his attack at middle and leg stump, probably bowling inswingers. As Imran delivers the first ball of the over, Botham moves his right foot outside the line of the leg stump. This enables him to hit a ball pitching on middle and leg stump through the covers. He swings the bat freely and the ball rockets through the vacant extra-cover region; there's no need to run and you simply stand there aghast at the brilliance of the shot. Botham stands still to receive the next delivery and sedately turns it down to long leg for a single. 187-4 in the 47th over. The next three balls from Imran are directed at leg stump. You play each one in the middle of the bat but succeed only in hitting the ball to one of the inner ring of fieldsmen on the leg side. With one ball of the over remaining you reason that a single is not much use since it would deprive Botham of the strike. You need a two, four or six. Do you opt

A. to step away to leg in order to emulate Botham's cover drive?

Or

B. stand still and continue trying to penetrate the leg-side field?

If **A** turn to page 86
If **B** turn to page 88

A. Having decided to ignore the intrusion, you stare at your toes for a while, then at Old Father Time up above the scoreboard, then a passing airplane, anything other than the streaker. None of these things seems to hold your attention, especially since the crowd keeps bursting into fits of laughter. As you glance at some of the Rest of the World's fieldsmen you also spot expressions of bewilderment upon their faces as well as great amusement. You become extremely curious. Finally your resolution snaps and you decide to turn around to see what is happening. However, it's too late. All you can see is a policeman leading the intruder, now wrapped in a cloak, off the field.

The opposition fieldsmen are all within earshot discussing the incident.

'I've never seen anything like that in my life before.'

'That was quite incredible.'

'This never happens in Bombay.'

'Amazing.'

At the other end Botham and Richards are laughing – obviously something to do with the interruption in play. As you settle into your stance to face another ball from Harper your curiosity is still at fever pitch. What was so remarkable about the streaker? Surely these guys are not entirely unacquainted with the female form? After all, most of them are married. Harper bowls. Why were they all so amazed? Gavaskar's eyes had nearly popped out of their sockets. What was it that you missed? Whilst all this is whizzing around your brain, one other thing that you miss, unfortunately, is the ball. By avoiding the interruption your concentration has been totally destroyed. You were speculating upon the recent incident rather than focusing on the ball. 155-5 and you are out for 17. No disgrace, but it could have been so much better. Back in the pavilion your curiosity is satisfied. Is that all it was about? What a waste of a wicket. In the middle Botham, now joined by Downton, presses on purposefully.

Turn to page 91

B. Before you know it Richards has bowled four 'dot' balls at you. He runs up from three paces and his gentle away-swingers pitch on middle and leg stump. Quite literally he bowls three balls in the same space of time that it takes many of his fast-bowling colleagues to bowl one. In addition his fielding off his own bowling is almost on a par with Roger Harper's. Your firm pushes towards long-on, which are designed to give Botham the strike against his former county colleague, are swiftly intercepted and within seconds Richards is in his delivery stride again. You are no more successful off the last two balls and Bill Frindall points out that 'Richards' maiden over, the first for 25 overs, was completed in just 97 seconds.' Fred Trueman responds that this was perfectly normal 'in my day'.

Between overs Botham warns you about letting Richards's overs slip by unnoticed and the momentum picks up just a little. Botham can pick up singles at will, but you are finding it rather more difficult, especially when Imran Khan is reintroduced into the attack. After 48 overs the score is 180-4 and Imran is to bowl to you. You fail to score off the first two balls of the over; the third ball is of good length, directed at off stump. Your firm cover drive is brilliantly stopped by Allan Border at short extra cover. Your frustrations mount. Border picks himself up and tosses the ball to Geoff Marsh, who is fielding at mid-off. Marsh, however, is distracted by some of the high jinks in the Tavern and isn't looking. The ball lobs over his head and rolls towards the pavilion. Border shouts at him. Botham looks to you. There's an easy single there if you want it. Do you

A. take the single and give Botham the strike? Or

B. reject the single on the grounds that it is contrary to the spirit of the game?

If **A** turn to page 85
If **B** turn to page 72

B. Why not enjoy the fun? Anyway she's making a bee-line for Botham so you are not going to be too exposed. Also you remember reading somewhere that it is important to switch off between deliveries; it's impossible to concentrate continuously for hours on end; much better to relax and enjoy the incident and then to switch back to the cricket at its conclusion.

A not unattractive blonde falls into Botham's arms; he pretends to tick her off for interrupting proceedings, gives her a quick peck on the cheek and a gentle pat with his Duncan Fearnley before she's led away by a blushing young police constable. The photographers, mindful of the following morning's front pages, are clicking frenetically and the cricket correspondent of one of the Sunday tabloids leaves his post up in the press box in search of an exclusive interview with the streaker. The crowd enjoy the interlude; indeed everyone seems to, except for the editor of BBC TV's cricket coverage, who wonders what to show.

Steady progress is maintained over the next few overs, Botham taking singles at will interspersed with the occasional boundary. However, you are finding it hard to get rid of the strike, especially after the reintroduction of Imran. After 48 overs the score is 180-4 and Imran is to bowl to you. You fail to score off the first two balls of the over; the third ball is of good length directed at off stump. Your firm cover drive is brilliantly stopped by Allan Border at extra cover. Your frustrations mount. Border picks himself up and tosses the ball towards Geoff Marsh at mid off. Marsh, however, is distracted by some of the high jinks in the Tavern and isn't looking. The ball lobs over his head and rolls towards the pavilion. Border shouts at him. Botham looks to you. There's an easy single there if you want it. Do you

A. take the single and give Botham the strike? Or

B. reject the single on the grounds that it is contrary to the spirit of the game?

If **A** turn to page 85
If **B** turn to page 72

Botham takes up the attack against Imran

B. 'No,' you bellow down the wicket. 'I don't want any charity; I'll get my runs properly, thank you very much.' At the other end Botham looks perplexed for a moment, shrugs his shoulders and strolls back to his crease. You notice that a broad grin spreads across Border's face; no doubt he is impressed by your magnanimity and you wonder whether to acknowledge him. Certainly you feel pretty magnanimous; after all you are very anxious to give the strike to Botham. However, you allow yourself briefly to speculate upon the tributes you must be receiving on the radio and TV. Indeed Brian Johnston expresses surprise and applauds your rejection of the single. On TV Ray Illingworth is less complimentary and declares that he would undoubtedly have taken the run.

Imran turns and begins his approach to the wicket, crouching low at first, then gradually straightening up as he reaches the stumps. The ball starts outside the off stump and you attempt another cover drive; however, it swings late and passes between bat and pad to send the middle stump cartwheeling towards Dujon. There's no point in looking back; your innings is over. As you head for the pavilion you see that Border still wears a wide grin and you begin to wonder if you hadn't been a little too generous to the opposition. If only you had taken that single you would still be batting. The line between good sportsmanship and naïvety is a thin one and maybe on this occasion you came down on the wrong side. The score is now 180-5 and your contribution of 24, whilst not spectacular, has helped to steady the innings. The members give you polite applause, whilst the players in the dressing room are more effusive. Thankfully none of them asks, 'Why ever didn't you take the single?' However, it is a question you keep asking yourself.

Out in the middle Downton takes guard and is soon scurrying up and down stealing runs – over the years he's studied Clive Radley – and he manages to give Botham a good proportion of the strike as England prepare for the final onslaught.

Turn to page 91

A. You make perfect contact and to your delight the ball races down to the Tavern, eluding even Roger Harper at square cover. Qadir is clearly annoyed at letting you off the hook and his concentration wavers; the third ball strays down the leg side and your fine sweep brings four more runs. Border withdraws his attacking fieldsmen and asks Harper 'to get loose' – surely an unnecessary request since Harper is permanently 'loose'. Off the last ball of the over you take a single to deep backward square leg. A good over for England and in the commentary box Trevor Bailey observes that the captain is playing 'very sensibly indeed' and that he looks a 'very fine player'.

At the mid-wicket conference you apologise to Gower for pinching the strike, but he quickly puts your mind at rest: 'Don't worry about that, old son. You keep going.'

In fact most professional batsmen are not too bothered if their partner keeps pinching the strike whilst Marshall is bowling.

The first three balls of Marshall's over are fast and straight; you meet all of them with the middle of the bat, but no runs are scored. However, you are pleased that you are adjusting to his pace and that you are picking up the ball much better than at the start of your innings. The fourth ball is short and you hook it – not a shot that you had planned; you simply reacted. The ball speeds down to the Mound Stand and Umpire Bird signals four runs. 129-3 in the 37th over.

The next ball is an inswinging yorker which you manage to keep out; Gower gives a nod of approval; even Marshall is impressed but he doesn't say so. The final ball is short and straight. Do you

A. sway out of the way? Or

B. attempt to play another hook shot?

If **A** turn to page 74
If **B** turn to page 76

A. You sway and, as the ball whistles past your nose, you feel very relieved that you opted not to hook. That was obviously his quicker bouncer. Gower comes down the wicket and observes: 'Marshall hits the bat hard, doesn't he?' 'Yes.'

Harper relieves Qadir at the Nursery End and Gower immediately decides to attack him. He comes down the wicket and drives him through extra cover for four; however, in trying to repeat the shot he fails to get to the pitch of the ball, which flies at knee height towards Geoff Marsh at square cover. Marsh takes off to his right and plucks the ball out of the air one-handed – a brilliant catch. Gower looks to the skies for a second, deftly tucks his bat under his shoulder and heads back to the pavilion, where a warm reception awaits him.

Out strides Botham swinging his massive Duncan Fearnley in an arc of 360 degrees. This is to loosen up his muscles as well as being a declaration of intent. Bars around the ground empty and there's an air of expectancy, though with Botham at the crease no one knows precisely what to expect. In fact he begins in remarkably subdued style; he plays out the rest of Harper's over quietly and when a leg-bye takes him up to Marshall's end he is content to 'see him off' since he's due for a break. He manages just a single to long leg, leaving him on strike against Harper. At your mid-wicket conference you contemplate telling him to 'get on with it', but you don't. To Botham Harper positions his mid-off and mid-on right on the boundary and from the first ball Botham sedately takes a single. 136-4 in the 40th over. However, when you're facing, he brings both these fielders up to save the single. You play the next two balls firmly to mid on without scoring. You wonder about the wisdom of hitting the ball 'over the top'. The next ball is given a little more air by Harper; it is straight and of fullish length. Do you
A. attempt a lofted drive over the mid-on and mid-off fieldsmen? Or
B. ensure that you drive the ball along the ground?

If **A** turn to page 78
If **B** turn to page 81

Is it time to attack Roger Harper?

B. The ball hits the top of your rib cage with a sickening thud; you gasp for breath and are thankful that Gower doesn't beckon you for a quick single because you don't feel you could make it to the other end. You wonder to what extent you should try to hide the pain. It was at times like this that Wes Hall used to console the batsman by revealing a wide toothy grin and shouting down to his victim: 'Rub it, man, 'cos I know it hurts.' Marshall, however, chooses to remain silent. He has made his point – you might be able to hook the slower bouncer, but not the quicker one. It is a point that Gower emphasises between overs, but there's really no need since the bruise will serve as a constant and effective reminder.

Harper replaces Qadir at the Nursery End and Gower promptly cover-drives him to the boundary; however, in trying to repeat the shot he fails to get to the pitch of the ball, which flies towards Geoff Marsh at square cover. Marsh dives to his right and the ball sticks in his hand – a brilliant catch. Gower looks to the skies, tucks his bat under his arm and sets off for the pavilion, where a warm reception awaits him. Botham strides out and the bars suddenly empty, just as they do at every cricketing venue around the world (except Karachi, Lahore and Faisalabad, etc. – no bars there). In fact Botham starts in subdued style. It takes him ten balls to get off the mark, a deflection to leg off Marshall, and there's some ironic slow handclapping from the Tavern. To Botham Harper places his mid-off and mid-on right on the boundary and from the first ball of the over Botham sedately takes a single. 136-4 in the 40th over. However when you're facing, he brings both these fieldsmen in to save the single. You play the next two balls firmly up to mid-on without scoring. Now you wonder about the wisdom of hitting the ball over the top. The next ball is given a little more air by Harper; it is straight and of fullish length. Do you

A. attempt a lofted drive over the bowler's head? Or

B. ensure that you drive the ball along the ground?

If **A** turn to page 78
If **B** turn to page 81

Botham begins his innings tentatively

A. On impact you lean back a little as you swing through the line of the ball and as you look up you see the ball sailing over the mid-on fieldsman and then crossing the boundary on the second bounce. It almost went for six! The crowd erupts with delight and above the applause Botham bellows his approval. After a swift consultation with his bowler Border tells his mid-on and mid-off to retreat to the boundary. Now there should be plenty of scope for singles.

This shot also seems to galvanise Botham, who is not prepared to let his skipper steal all the limelight. In the next over he lofts Reid who has replaced Marshall at the Pavilion End to the long-off boundary and suddenly the Rest of the World are on the defensive. Botham is now warming to his task and clearly has confidence in his partner since he doesn't try to monopolise the strike, whilst you are timing the ball as sweetly as at any time in your career. What a day to find your best form! After 45 overs the score has moved on to 171-4 and Harper, bowling to a packed on-side field, is about to continue. His main aim now is the prevention of boundaries; he is prepared to concede singles.

Botham greets the first ball of the over with a reverse sweep, beautifully executed. You are amazed that a colossus like Botham should play with such delicacy. The ball speeds away to the third-man boundary and Harper, normally so unemotional on the field, looks utterly deflated. With an orthodox on-drive Botham takes a single from the next ball. 176-4 in the 46th over. You fail to score off the next three deliveries, which are directed at middle and leg stump, and you sense that Harper is recovering his composure. It occurs to you that another reverse sweep would destroy his confidence completely as well as getting the scoreboard moving again. However, it is a risky shot. As Harper approaches the crease do you opt
A. to play a reverse-sweep shot? Or
B. to be content to play the ball in an orthodox manner?

If **A** turn to page 80
If **B** turn to page 87

Bruce Reid of Australia attempts to subdue Botham

A. As Harper delivers the ball you push out your right leg eighteen inches to get into position for the reverse sweep. The ball is straight, quicker than normal and of yorker length, giving you no room to play the shot. You are in a desperate tangle as the ball thuds into your pad. Harper wheels around in mid air and leaps to the sky as he appeals to Umpire Shepherd. He wants justice; you can't have any Tom, Dick or Harry upsetting the off-spinner's craft with reverse-sweep shots. Shepherd pauses; the crowd is hushed for a second; you disentangle yourself and look down the wicket to be greeted by the cry of 'That's out' augmented by the dreaded raised finger. Harper is jubilant and you set off for the pavilion. The score is 176-5, last man 32.

In the commentary box the pundits praise a bright and breezy innings. One of them calls it a 'little gem', which pleases your mother but they all add that it was an unnecessary dismissal. Fred Trueman says, 'I can't for the life of me understand what he was trying to do,' and recalls that in his day the England captain would never have attempted such a shot.

Meanwhile you are cursing yourself even as the members grant you a warm reception in the Long Room. You had been playing so well. Why bother to complicate batting or try to emulate Botham? Everthing had been going so well that you had become over-confident and had tried to be too clever. Back in the dressing room your team-mates congratulate you without any comment about your mode of dismissal. You wonder whether the Chairman will be so understanding and you muse upon what might have been.

Out in the middle Downton has already taken guard and is soon into his stride scampering singles and giving Botham as much of the strike as possible as England prepare for the final onslaught.

Please turn to page 91

B. Again the ball goes straight to mid-on and there's no run. Border shouts 'Well bowled, mate' to his off-spinner, clearly relieved that an over, which had started so ominously, had ended so sedately and you begin to wonder whether your decision has let slip the initiative. At the Pavilion End Marshall is replaced by Reid and Botham decides to launch an attack against the gangling left-armer. He hits two sizzling boundaries, which prompts Border to keep the minimum of four fielders in the ring when Botham is on strike, cover point, extra cover, mid-off and mid-wicket. However, when you are on strike two more fielders reinforce the infield and you find it very difficult to pierce them. Indeed throughout the next three overs out of the fourteen runs scored your contribution is just two singles. You grow increasingly restless and so do some of the spectators in the Tavern. Encouraged by several pints of best bitter, albeit in plastic cups, they break out into ironic applause when you scramble a single at the beginning of the 45th over, taking the score to 163-4. Botham tells you not to worry about them and that your timing will return, though you're not sure whether he really believes this. Certainly Botham seems unaffected by their jeering since he smashes the next two deliveries from Reid over mid-off, whereupon Border instructs mid-off to stay on the boundary. Clearly he wants his bowlers to bowl as many balls as possible at you since Botham is on the verge of running riot. 171-4 in the 45th over. All around the ground now there is great excitement and hubbub as Reid runs up to the wicket. Botham plays a ferocious cover drive which flies in the air towards Richards at extra cover. The West Indian captain takes off to his right and plucks the ball out of the air with his right hand and once he's regained his balance he hurls the ball up into the heavens out of sheer delight at catching his former county colleague. Botham astounded by the catch sets off towards you and the pavilion. Do you

A. commiserate with him as he approaches? Or

B. run up to the other end?

If **A** turn to page 82
If **B** turn to page 84

A. Your 'Bad luck, Ian' receives a lukewarm response. Botham stares in disbelief at Richards, he glances at you and then looks up at the players' balcony, where something odd is happening. John Emburey is jumping up and down in a state of remarkable animation. He is waving his arms frantically and, once he has caught Botham's attention, he starts shouting – in vain – it's impossible to hear him above the crowd. Next he points his arm towards square leg. The two batsmen turn in that direction and see David Shepherd, immobile like a guard at Buckingham Palace, with his arm outstretched – the signal for a no-ball. Suddenly it clicks. As the last ball was bowled only three fieldsmen were inside the inner circle, which was why David Shepherd had called 'No-ball'. Because of the din nobody had heard him. Botham sheepishly returns to the popping crease as the fielding side recognise what has happened. Border is furious with himself. Reid is furious with Border. In fact Botham, though relieved to have escaped dismissal, is none too pleased with you. He has been made to look a little stupid and he asks, 'Why didn't you signal to me that there were only three in the circle? I could have had an almighty slog. You should be looking out for that.' You resist telling him that he seemed to have had an almighty slog anyway.

Botham makes the most of his good fortune and you manage to square-cut a loose ball from Harper to the boundary. Border responds by bringing back Imran at the Pavilion End; he places five men on the leg side, obviously intent on a leg-stump attack. Botham steps away to leg and crashes the first ball to the vacant extra-cover boundary – a breathtaking shot. Standing still to the next he sedately takes a single. 187-4 in the 47th over. You play the next three balls into the leg side without penetrating the infield. With just one ball left you recognise that a single is not much use since it will deprive Botham of the strike. Do you

A. step away to leg to try to emulate Botham's cover drive? Or

B. stand still and try to penetrate the leg-side field?

If **A** turn to page 86
If **B** turn to page 88

Imran Khan in full flight

B. You set off for the striker's end shouting 'Run, you fool'. Botham is totally bemused by your behaviour and continues his leisurely stroll towards the pavilion. Once you've made your ground you turn to see Botham's ample backside slowly receding into the distance. You yell out, almost plaintively, 'Come back, Ian.' Botham, clearly confused, turns and looks quizzically in your direction, whereupon you decide that the simplest method of explanation is to point towards the square-leg umpire. Botham looks at David Shepherd, who is standing there resolutely with his arm outstretched, the signal for a no-ball. Suddenly he grasps what has happened; since there were only three men in the circle at the moment of delivery the umpire had called a no-ball, but his shout had been drowned by the din of the crowd. Instead of Botham's being dismissed, the awareness of his captain has pinched him an extra single. A trifle embarrassed, Botham turns around and goes back to the middle, whilst the fielding side, who had all been celebrating his dismissal, realise themselves what has happened. Botham comes down the wicket to you. 'Good thinking there, skip.' And then he bellows a few words to Allan Border, his Queensland captain. Whatever is said seems to amuse Botham himself rather more than Border.

Confidence restored you loft Harper for a boundary in the next over and Border opts to bring back Imran Khan, who places five men on the leg side, so is clearly intent upon attacking the leg stump. As Imran delivers his first ball, Botham steps away to leg and crashes the ball to the vacant extra-cover boundary – a breathtaking shot. By more orthodox means he takes a single next ball. 187-4 in the 47th over. The next three balls are all directed at middle and leg stump and even though you middle them you are unable to penetrate the leg-side cordon. With just one ball left in the over you recognise that a single is not much use since it will deprive Botham of the strike. Do you

A. step away to leg to try to emulate the Botham cover drive? Or

B. try to penetrate the leg-side field?

If **A** turn to page 86
If **B** turn to page 88

A. You tiptoe down to the other end to complete the single. The crowd are highly amused, but Border isn't. He is snarling, though you are not sure whether the snarl is directed at you or Geoff Marsh. Botham flicks the next ball off his legs and it lands in the fourteenth row of the Mound Stand. While the ball is being retrieved he assures you that you were quite right to take the single. Not for the first time today you are reminded that this isn't a benefit match.

Now you play some of the best strokes of your innings, bringing boundaries off both Qadir and Richards, who are sharing the overs at the Nursery End. Even though you have been batting for an hour and a half, a long innings by your standards, you don't feel at all tired. You are enjoying yourself far too much for that.

With the score at 220-4 and your personal total 45 you drive the first ball of the 55th over to the sightscreen. The crowd roars its approval and you realise that you only need a single to complete your fifty. A fifty on your debut for England! Before the match you didn't dare dream of such a thing.

You play the next ball square on the off-side and set off for a single. Botham responds. However, after a few strides you recognise that the fieldsman is Harper so you bellow 'No'. Botham dutifully slams on the brakes, but in doing so slips over and falls to the ground in the middle of the wicket, stranded like a beached whale. You are almost close enough to shake hands with him. Harper is about to throw the ball to the wicket-keeper and it is clear that one of you is going to have to go and it is your decision since Botham is still immobile on the grass. Do you

A. run past Botham to the safety of the non-striker's end? Or

B. decide not to cross thereby ensuring that you will be the dismissed batsman, one run away from a coveted fifty?

If **A** turn to page 93
If **B** turn to page 90

A. Imran sets off from his mark crouching low at first and then gradually gaining height like an Olympic sprinter. As you step away to the leg side he bowls a full-length ball at off stump; at the end of its journey the ball swings in and passes the inside of your flailing bat to knock the leg stump out of the ground. There's no point in looking round, so you set off straightaway for the pavilion. As you pass Botham he gives you a consoling pat on the back. The members in the pavilion give you a warm reception, but not as warm as the players in the dressing room.

As you sip the squash that the attendant has promptly placed by your cricket bag, you begin to wonder whether you hadn't been a little overambitious. It's one thing to take the attack to the slower bowlers, another to Imran. You've discovered the hard way that not everyone can bat like Botham.

Still, the score is now 187-5 and your contribution of 31, whilst not Man of the Match material, has certainly helped to steady the innings. None the less it's a pity that you didn't decide just to play that last Imran delivery rather than go for glory, since there are more than ten overs left.

The balcony is now crowded as the innings enters its final stages. Dilley has forsaken his Walkman now, Edmonds his phone. Emburey, the next man in, is practising a few textbook cover drives in the mirror, the likes of which he's yet to play in the middle.

Outside, Paul Downton has already taken guard and is scurrying up and down the wicket stealing runs – over the years he has studied Clive Radley – and he manages to give Botham a good proportion of the strike as England prepare for the final onslaught.

Turn to page 91

B. The ball pitches on leg stump and you turn it to deep backward square leg for an easy single. You wonder whether you've let Harper off the hook but at your mid-wicket conference Botham stresses that there's no point in taking any unnecessary risks at this stage. 'Leave the reverse-sweeping to me.' The next time he is on strike he charges Reid, halts and then late-cuts him and you assume that this shot must constitute a 'necessary risk' in Botham's book.

During the next two overs runs flow easily. Botham is playing with complete freedom and you've never batted better. However, the return of Imran gives Border the much-needed breakthrough when Botham having been smashed on the toe by the previous ball is bowled by an inswinging yorker. 202-5 in the 49th over. The crowd gives him a warm reception; they are disappointed to see the end of his innings. So are you; it had been so easy to bat with him since there was no pressure to score quickly and his sheer presence had put the bowlers in a more defensive frame of mind. Now you recognise that you must take on the dominant role whilst Paul Downton establishes himself at the crease. However, in one sense you enjoy this new responsibility. You are in charge, the senior partner, and you give yourself freedom to go for your shots. An on-drive off Imran gives you the greatest pleasure and at the beginning of the 54th over, which is to be bowled by Abdul Qadir, the score is 222-5. You realise that you are on 49, one run away from a memorable maiden half century. Not even in your dreams had you contemplated scoring 50 on this afternoon.

Qadir's second delivery is a poor one, just what you need – short of a length, in fact a rare long hop. Do you opt

A. to play it on the leg side for a single, thereby bringing you to a coveted 50? Or

B. do you go for a full-blooded pull shot in the general direction of Old Father Time?

If **A** turn to page 89
If **B** turn to page 92

B. You decide to stand still and play the ball in an orthodox manner, which is probably just as well since Imran bowls a vicious inswinging yorker. It would have been very difficult to hit that one to the extra-cover boundary. In between overs Botham stresses that there's still plenty of time to go and there's no need to do anything daft. Next ball he attempts another reverse sweep.

During the next six overs the scoreboard ticks over steadily at a rate of five an over, mostly through singles, as the Rest of the World's bowlers draw upon all their experience. Border shrewdly shuffles them around, using the pacemen from the Pavilion End and a mixture of Qadir and Richards at the other. Your mouth is dry now; after all you've been batting for twenty overs, an hour and a half's play; however, you don't feel at all tired; you are enjoying yourself too much for that. With the score at 220-4 and your personal total 45 you drive the first ball of the 55th over to the sightscreen. The crowd roars its approval and you realise that you only need a single to complete your fifty. A fifty on your debut for England! Before the match you didn't dare dream of such a thing.

You play the next ball square on the off side and set off for a single. Botham responds. However, after a few strides you recognise that the fieldsman is Harper so you bellow 'No'. Botham dutifully slams on the brakes, but in doing so slips over and falls to the ground in the middle of the wicket, stranded like a beached whale. You are almost close enough to shake hands with him. Harper is about to throw the ball to the wicket-keeper and it is clear that one of you is going to have to go and it is your decision since Botham is still immobile on the grass. Do you

A. run past Botham to the safety of the non-striker's end? Or

B. decide not to cross thereby ensuring that you will be the dismissed batsman, one run away from a coveted fifty?

If **A** turn to page 93
If **B** turn to page 90

A. You hit the ball to the right of the mid-wicket fieldsman and set off for the run that will take your score to fifty. As you pass Downton you hear the dreaded words 'hurry up' and glancing to your left you realise to your horror that the mid-wicket fieldsman is the ubiquitous Harper. As he is about to pick up the ball you strain every muscle in your body for extra speed before diving headlong for the crease like an aircraft crash-landing in a muddy field. As you stretch out your bat the ball breaks the wicket and there's a thunderous appeal. Umpire Shepherd is perfectly placed square of the wicket and gives his decision.

Up in the commentary box Richie Benaud is on air: 'My word. What a superb piece of umpiring that was by David Shepherd.' and, as he studies the action-replay along with millions of other viewers, 'That was so close.'

Down on the pitch you drag yourself to your feet and dust yourself off; you are covered by a mixture of loose soil and grass stains; your pads look as though you've just completed a game of hockey on a wet February afternoon. The crowd applauds and you raise your bat as the scoreboard shows 50 under the no. 5 batsman. It was not the most dignified manner in which to reach the landmark but that doesn't seem to matter now. Paul Downton comes down the wicket, shakes your hand and says 'Well played, skip. Keep going now' and on the balcony the rest of your team emerge to clap their congratulation. Even Allan Border, who's been distinctly stand-offish since you parted company after the toss says 'Played, mate'.

Downton now attacks Qadir with two successive boundaries from an extra-cover drive and a sweep before being bowled attempting to cut Qadir's googly, taking the score to 231-6 from 54 overs. He is replaced by his Middlesex colleague John Emburey.

Turn to page 94

B. You turn around and start running towards Dujon, a token gesture since there's no way that you can regain your ground. The wicket-keeper deftly removes one bail and you complete yet another U-turn. Botham is still grovelling around on the pitch and on your way back to the pavilion you stretch out your hand to help him to his feet. He says 'Thanks', though you're not certain whether he is referring to your helping hand or your self-sacrifice. You mutter something suitably selfless like 'Keep going'. You are extremely disappointed to be out one run short of a half century, especially through a needless run-out; however you feel a little better after receiving a rousing reception as you leave the field. In addition you know deep down that you made the right decision since realistically Botham is rather more likely to wreak havoc in the final overs than you are.

As you enter the dressing room there's a chorus of 'Bad lucks' and 'Well playeds' as the attendant brings you a glass of squash, which you drink in two gulps. Undoubtedly your colleagues have been impressed by your batting and also by your good sense in sacrificing your wicket. As you unbuckle your pads you hear the roar of the crowd as Botham strikes an enormous six, another vindication of your decision.

In the 57th over Botham is caught on the square-leg boundary, making the score 249-6, leaving the tail to do their best, though they are unable to maintain Botham's strike-rate, which is hardly surprising. In the penultimate over Emburey considers himself very unlucky to be caught on the square-cover boundary after playing one of his shots, the inside-out slash-drive minus back-lift. In the same over Gavaskar nonchalantly clings on to a skier to dismiss Downton and off the last ball of the innings Edmonds is run out, whilst still trying to maintain his dignity. The final score is 264-9 and Dilley is relieved not to have to bat.

Please turn to page 96

The Chairman comes over to say 'Well played' and adds that the game is nicely poised before he is 'dragged' off for a drink in the committee room. As you unstrap your pads you find it relatively easy to interpret what is happening on the field from the reaction of the crowd, which is becoming more animated every over. The 200 comes up in the 51st over and is greeted by enthusiastic applause. However, at the end of the 55th over with the score at 227-5 Botham is bowled by Reid as he attempts to hit him towards Paddington Station. He marches off the field, clearly annoyed with himself, but he's cooled off by the time he has completed the long trek back to the dressing room and upon arrival he shouts across the room: 'Sorry, skip. Missed it.'

You are far from annoyed for you recognise that his half century has restored an innings which had looked like crumbling away at the fall of the fourth wicket.

The last five overs of the innings produce another 37 runs. Emburey, with no back-lift and looking tentative, to say the least, against the faster bowlers, still contrives to hit three boundaries, one a remarkable sliced six into an astonished Tavern. Downton continues to scurry between the wickets. Marshall claims two well deserved victims and off the last ball of the innings Edmonds is run out, whilst still trying to maintain his dignity. The final score is 264-9 and Dilley is relieved not to have to bat.

It could have been a lot worse.

Turn to page 96

B. Your bat meets the ball with a healthy crack as you execute the pull shot. On the mid-wicket boundary Martin Crowe, his eyes fixed on the ball, sprints like an All-Black wing three-quarter, but to no avail. The ball flies over his head into the second tier of the stand. Umpire Shepherd signals six, unnecessarily really, since the scorers had been watching the ball's flight with some concern; at one point it seemed destined for the scorebox itself. The crowd erupts with spontaneous applause celebrating your half century for they like to see someone reach this landmark with style. As Paul Downton comes down the wicket to offer congratulations, you acknowledge their applause by raising your bat. Allan Border, who has been distinctly stand-offish since you parted company after the toss, says 'Played, mate' and the players' balcony outside the dressing room is full with your colleagues clapping their congratulation.

In the Radio 3 commentary box Brian Johnston talks of an 'absolutely splendid innings' before seeking expert analysis from Trevor Bailey, who observes that the English captain has played 'very, very, sensibly indeed', whereupon Bill Frindall, anxious to atone, furnishes listeners with precise details of your innings. An inebriated supporter staggers on to the pitch, trailing a Union Jack behind him, to offer personal congratulations. On air 'Johnners' fills in time by informing listeners of a benefit match on 4 September at Seaton for an extremely worthy cause, until finally Qadir resumes the over.

You play the ball carefully and there is no run; the next ball is outside off stump and you late-cut it delicately for three; the crowd purrs with delight; you are really enjoying this now. However you quickly come back to the harsh realities of the game when Downton attempts to cut Qadir's googly and is bowled by the last ball of the over. The score is now 231-6 from 54 overs and the new batsman is John Emburey.

Turn to page 94

A. Dujon gently removes one bail and promptly replaces it. Botham, still on the ground, looks horrified. He is not accustomed to being run out. He drags himself to his feet, dusts himself off and slowly heads towards the pavilion. You are not quite sure where to look. As he passes you, you pluck up courage to glance in his direction; however his eyes are fixed straight ahead and either he doesn't hear or he chooses to ignore your 'Sorry about that, Ian'. The crowd gives him a standing ovation tinged with sympathy as he strides unsmilingly up the pavilion steps. You begin to wonder whether you reacted in the right way; perhaps England's cause might have been better served if Botham rather than yourself were still at the crease. Back in the pavilion Botham vents his fury, though Allan Lamb cannot avoid seeing the funny side of the whole episode, observing that milk could turn quicker than England's greatest all-rounder.

In the middle you are joined by Paul Downton who plays out the rest of the over. As you prepare to face the next one, bowled by Reid, you are still considering what you should say to Botham when you get back inside. You attempt to turn the ball on the leg side, but succeed only in getting an outside edge. You have no idea where the ball has gone but Downton calls for a single as it trickles down to third man. The crowd acknowledges your fifty and you raise your bat. Downton takes another single and in your perplexed state you decide that you should try to accelerate Botham-style since you've just run him out. He would be smashing boundaries now so you should do the same. You attempt to swing the ball to the vacant mid-wicket area – unsuccessfully – and the ball shatters the stumps. 226-6.

As you approach the pavilion the crowd applaud, but you recognise that your reception is less wholehearted than that given to Botham a few minutes earlier. You are surprised that it is possible to feel so lukewarm about scoring a fifty at Lord's. You would have felt much happier if you had sacrificed your wicket on 49 and left Botham to get on with it.

In the dressing room your players congratulate you, though Lamb is still trying to contain his giggling. Botham, it transpires, is having a shower. As you unbuckle your pads and gulp down some squash, you await his return somewhat uneasily, still wondering what to say – just as you were when you tried to heave Reid out of the ground. Minutes later the door swings open and Botham, dripping wet, enters and heads towards you.

Please turn to page 95

Marshall is brought back into the attack to bowl his final three overs and Emburey raises his eyebrows as if to say, 'It's just my luck that I should have to bat when Marshall's bowling.' He struggles initially to get the ball away. Then out of the blue he plays one of his shots, the inside-out slash-drive minus back-lift, and the ball sails into the Mound Stand much to the consternation of Bruce Reid. In the same over he attempts to repeat the shot only to be caught, rather unfortunately, on the square-cover boundary. Up go the eyebrows again. 244-7 from 57 overs. Boundaries are hard to come by now. When you are on strike every fielder concedes a single. The statutory four fielders loiter right on the edge of the ring. It is hard for you to believe that the opposition, which is made up of the best cricketers in the world, are affording you such respect. So are your own players.

Off the last ball of the penultimate over Foster runs himself out in an effort to ensure that you will be facing the last one, which is bowled by Imran Khan. 254-8. You drive the first ball of the over firmly to long-on for one run. Now Edmonds has an exploratory – and unsuccessful – swish and you advise him to push for a single, which he does. Unfortunately the ball goes straight to Richards at extra cover. 'And there is no run' states Henry Blofeld emphatically. You are relieved when Edmonds manages to scramble a single next ball. Two balls left. You now decide to back away to leg and you scythe the ball wide of third man for two. Edmonds however attempts a third with the enthusiasm and the optimism of a nine-year-old and he has no chance of beating Dujon's throw. In the pavilion Dilley groans; he has to go out for one ball. He trudges out and upon arrival at the bowler's end declares that he'll be running come what may. This time you choose to move towards the off side and you flick a full-length ball effortlessly off your legs. There is no need for Dilley to run as it lands in row 12 of the Mound Stand. At the end of the innings the score is 264-9. You are 74 not out and the crowd gives you a standing ovation.

Turn to page 96

He pauses and you begin to open your mouth, though as yet there is no sound. Sensing your anguish, Botham, while obviously still pained by his dismissal, manages to say: 'Don't worry about it; these things happen.' Lamb shouts: 'Feeling better for a shower, Nijinsky?' and everyone laughs.

Outside Downton and Emburey are trying to plunder every possible run from the final overs. To everyone's amazement Emburey contrives to slice Reid over square cover for six, but is bowled trying to repeat the shot next ball. 251-7 from 58 overs. In the penultimate over Downton skies Marshall and Gavaskar at square cover takes a fine running catch and off the final ball of the innings Edmonds is run out, whilst still trying to maintain his dignity. The final score is 264-9 and Dilley is relieved not to have to bat.

Turn to page 96

ENGLAND BOWLING

The ten minutes between innings is scarcely long enough for the fielding side especially for those who have just been batting; they have to wrench off their shirts, wipe themselves down with a towel, grab a quick drink and put on some fresh kit. The fast bowlers carefully tie up their bowling boots, tight enough to give sufficient support without harming the circulation. Indeed, top fast bowlers tend their boots as lovingly as opening batsmen do their bats. Dilley's right boot has a gleaming silver drag plate to prevent it disintegrating after his first spell. Botham has carved a small hole at the end of his boot to stop his big toe from rubbing. Foster is strapping on a corset underneath his shirt, a legacy from previous back problems. Downton has already put on his minuscule keeping pads and is throwing a ball from glove to glove. Gooch shouts for some tape to hide an advertising logo on his trousers. Lamb wants some chewing gum – if he's fielding on the boundary there will be no one to talk to so his mouth will need something to do. Athey combs his hair; Gower thinks about it, but doesn't bother. Edmonds puts on his watch. In the TV commentary position Tony Lewis runs through the fall of the nine wickets with the assistance of Ray Illingworth. In the press box several of the journalists study their television monitors carefully; it is just possible that they may have missed one or two of the dismissals whilst replenishing their glasses. Illingworth believes that the game is beautifully poised. Even though 264 is a good score by any standards, this is a good wicket and England will have to be at their best to win.

Those in the stands stretch their legs and contemplate getting a drink but most think better of it as long queues are already forming. It is a time for the spectators to relax a little since the action so far has demanded their constant attention.

Back in the dressing room there is little time for you to relax. From now on your mind must be razor-sharp and some decisions have to be made before you enter the playing area. You sidle over to Graham Dilley who is stretching his hamstrings on the table.

'I'd like you to start from the Pavilion End, please.'

'Right.' A suitably monosyllabic reply from your fast bowler. A quick discussion about field placings establishes that he'll start with two slips and a gully. One key to success in limited-overs matches is taking early wickets therefore it is vital to have some close fielders ready to catch the edges whilst the ball is new and most likely to swing. You move around to Neil Foster and tell him that he'll have the second over from the Nursery End. There was a time when Botham would have been deeply insulted not to have the new ball, but now he's quite content to bowl at a slightly reduced pace later on. He nods approvingly when you inform him of your strategy.

Next you have a word with your spinners asking which ends they prefer. The slope at Lord's is far steeper than it appears on television and you are fortunate that both your spinners have spent their careers at Middlesex and know how to make the necessary adjustments. They both declare that they can bowl at either end, which is a relief to you. However, traditionally, the slope has meant that the off-spinner usually bowls at the Pavilion End, the left-armer at the Nursery End and whilst you are prepared to be flexible you state that they'll probably begin their spells at their usual ends. Emburey points out that with two spinners in the attack it might be worthwhile introducing one of them relatively early in the innings to prevent a situation where you have no alternative to spin late in the innings when 'the slog is on'. The bell clangs and you decide that you ought to say something to the whole side. Amongst such a band of experienced professionals there's no point in being too schoolmasterly, just a few words to establish that it's time to go. It is not a memorable speech nor an original one: 'Every run is vital . . . Encourage the bowlers . . . We can do it . . . Good luck.' It's a relief to all concerned when someone shouts: 'They're out there.' It's time to go.

Out of the door and down two flights of stairs; you turn around just once to check that the others are coming. They are there, Gower, Gooch, Edmonds and Botham all dutifully following you, the captain of England. In the Long Room the members rise, at least those who can complete this manoeuvre without assistance do, and they create a tunnel to the doorway. As you step out on to the turf you look up and breathe in deeply as if trying to inhale the atmosphere for good. It is a moment you would like to have with you for the rest of your life. The crowd applauds enthusiastically and there are a few cheers – or are they jeers – from the Tavern. As you head for the middle Dilley and Foster sprint past you eager to mark out their run-ups and to loosen up. Umpire Bird throws you the new ball, which you toss to Downton. He throws gentle catches to those around him for even the most experienced of players are anxious to have a feel of the ball.

Warm applause heralds the entrance of Gavaskar and Marsh. On top of the Warner Stand Tony Lewis points out that 'Gavaskar is the shorter of the two with the floppy hat, which hides his individually designed skull-cap. Marsh is wearing the familiar green helmet of Australia' but for most viewers this information is redundant. They know who the openers are.

Certainly Dilley does. Over the years, previous encounters have ensured that he has a healthy respect for both of them. Gavaskar takes guard, runs up and down on the spot right up on his toes and then surveys the field: two slips, a gully, cover, mid-off, mid-on, square leg, third man and long leg. You opt to field at first slip; after all that was where Brearley stood and they say that he read the game reasonably well from there.

You glance around the field just to check that everyone is positioned where you want them and Dilley sets off. Gavaskar allows the first ball to pass harmlessly outside the off stump. Dilley has not yet reached full pace and his first objective is to establish control of his line and length. He knows that Gavaskar is immensely strong off his legs so he aims to bowl on or outside the off stump. However, the last ball of the over is directed at middle and leg stump and is clipped effortlessly to the square-leg boundary. The power of the shot is astonishing, one deft flick of the wrists and the ball crosses the rope by the Mound Stand. Gavaskar doesn't contemplate running. Dilley looks and, no doubt, feels wronged. Umpire Bird signals four and calls 'Over'. From long leg Foster marches up to Umpire Shepherd like a fresh-faced Sandhurst cadet. Marsh is watchful, but untroubled, and gets off the mark with a firm push to extra cover.

From first slip you can see that Dilley, in particular, is managing to make the ball swing away from the bat and in his third over he passes the outside edge of Marsh's bat twice in succession. Otherwise the openers proceed without too much difficulty, Gavaskar missing nothing off his legs, whilst Marsh is eager to attack anything wide of the off stump. After eight overs the score is 31-0 and you decide to give Dilley one more over. Marsh playing a little away from his body pushes the first ball through extra cover for two. He plays and misses at the second, drives the third firmly but straight to mid-off and then smashes the fourth to the cover boundary. 37-0 in the 9th over. Runs are coming a little too freely for your liking but Dilley is still managing to swing the odd delivery. It occurs to you that your second slip might be moved to extra cover to try to stem the run-rate. Do you

A. go to extra cover yourself, leaving Botham as the only slip fieldsman? Or

B. keep the field the same until the end of the over?

If **A** turn to page 100
If **B** turn to page 103

A. You trot to extra cover and feel that your decision is justified when Marsh drives the ball straight to you. However, off the last ball of the over the Australian attempts another cover drive; the ball clips the outside edge of the bat and flies through the vacant second-slip area at catchable height. Botham dives despairingly and Dilley looks to the heavens as the ball is tossed back by a member of the ground staff at the Nursery End. Dilley takes his sweater and heads for long leg contemplating what might have been. One more over from Foster yields three runs and you decide upon a double change – Emburey from the Pavilion End and Botham from his favoured Nursery End.

Emburey immediately finds his rhythm and begins with a much-appreciated maiden to Marsh. He even manages to turn a couple of deliveries down the slope. In his second over Marsh, anxious to break the shackles, comes down the wicket to drive but the flight of the ball deceives him and he hits it firmly but in the air to mid-wicket where Gower accepts the catch. 48-1 and a much-needed breakthrough. Emburey is delighted and you cheer up a bit as well since your ill-fated field change hasn't proved too costly. However, any euphoria is tempered by the sight of Viv Richards strolling to the crease. He isn't looking terribly apprehensive and why should he? His record in Lord's finals is phenomenal; it is his favourite stage. There are four balls left in the over. Up to now Emburey has been bowling to a conventional one-day field with six men on the leg side and no close catchers. In conversation with Emburey you toy with the idea of placing two men close to the wicket on each side of the batsman at short leg and silly point for the rest of the over in order to place unusual pressure on the West Indian captain. Emburey is not sure and leaves the decision to you.

A. If you choose to post two close catchers turn to page 102

B. If you choose to keep a conventional one-day field turn to page 104

Geoff Marsh misjudges a cover drive and . . .

A. Richards is surprised by such confidence, even insolence, whilst Emburey, a miser with the ball, is still unsure about the wisdom of the move. He has been on the receiving end of a Richards onslaught before. The West Indian plays his first ball tentatively with a dead bat. To the second he comes down the wicket and drives the ball in the air, just clearing the outstretched arms of Gooch at mid-on – so near to a catch. His third ball, however, is more likely to provide catching practice for Gooch's wife who is sitting innocently in Q stand, an awesome stroke. Richards clearly does not want to suffer the indignity of having fielders hovering around the bat any longer. Emburey comes over to you to suggest that the field be adjusted and you agree to the removal of Athey and Gower from short leg and silly point. To the last ball of the over Richards plays a forward defensive stroke with exaggerated care and there's a hint of a smile as he ambles down the wicket.

At the other end Botham relishes the challenge of bowling to his two former county colleagues. He is anxious to impress them with his new, economical style. Both Gavaskar and Richards remain subdued against him not wanting to lose their personal battles with their friend and rival. Gavaskar, in particular, withdraws into his shell for a while. It is Richards who breaks the deadlock by flicking a short-of-a-length ball over square leg for six. 71-1 in the 18th over. Botham immediately asks for Gooch at square leg to be positioned on the boundary and the next ball he runs up to the crease a little quicker and pounds the ball into the wicket. Richards goes for the hook but misjudges the change of pace; the ball having hit the top edge of the bat balloons up into the air between Dilley at long leg and Gooch. It is unclear who is best placed to take the catch, which would result in the prized wicket of Richards. As captain do you

A. let the two fielders concerned sort out who is to attempt the catch? Or

B. shout the christian name of the fielder, who you think is best placed to catch the ball?

If **A** turn to page 111
If **B** turn to page 108

B. Marsh pushes the next ball confidently into the gap at extra cover for two more runs. Now Dilley suggests that you should remove a slip fielder but, since there is just one ball left of the over, you leave the field unchanged. The next ball is a full-length away-swinger wide of off stump. Marsh again attacks the ball but this time he has to stretch and succeeds only in getting a thick outside edge. The ball flies off to Botham's right at second slip. In a rapid reflex-action Botham removes his right hand from his right knee and the next thing you know he is clutching the ball inches above the ground. Dilley is jubilant and rushes up to congratulate his Worcester colleague. Once he has done that he comes over to acknowledge his captain's wisdom; certainly you have gained his confidence for a while. The score is 39-1 as Vivian Richards enters his favourite stage.

Richards proudly wears his West Indian sweater and cap – one of the few players in the match to shun the helmet – and once in the middle he flexes his muscles ominously. At the other end you decide to introduce Botham. He is obviously keen to bowl to his two former colleagues, anxious to convince them that he has mastered his new economical style. In addition neither batsman wants to be dismissed by him, such is their friendly rivalry. So the run-rate slows.

Dilley bowls one more over and is then replaced by Emburey at the Pavilion End. He commands respect but with the batsmen taking few risks doesn't look like making the breakthrough. Both Gavaskar and Richards are content with three or four singles an over from the off-spinner, mostly from firm drives to long-on. Botham meanwhile is displaying uncharacteristic patience and is thoroughly enjoying 'being boring'. However, even though the batsmen are being restricted, you are becoming increasingly anxious since either player could change gear at any time. 61-1 after eighteen overs. You desperately need a wicket.

Turn to page 105

B. Richards begins sedately, content to pick up singles from the off-spinner. Emburey is happier with a deep-set field. He has endured a Richards onslaught several times in one-day internationals so he doesn't mind conceding singles from drives to long-on. Each man has a deep respect for the other's skill and the duel is a little like the opening rounds of a boxing match, an analogy that Richards would enjoy. Neither is prepared to commit himself to all-out attack.

At the Nursery End Botham is enjoying himself bowling to his two former colleagues. He doesn't strive for too much pace, but concentrates on maintaining a consistent line and length; he wants to prove to the batsmen that he has acquired the virtue of patience in his old age. Neither batsman thinks that his self-discipline can last indefinitely so both sit back and wait for a loose ball. However, for the moment Botham keeps them waiting.

You are relieved that a measure of control has been achieved after the Rest of the World's brisk start, but you also recognise that you have a few problems. When are you going to introduce Edmonds into the attack? He's clearly anxious to get into the game and you can't leave his overs too late in the innings, yet Botham is doing such a good job at the Nursery End that you are tempted to keep him going for a while. Who is going to replace Emburey at the Pavilion End? Also, whilst the run-rate has slowed appreciably the Rest of the World are not yet under any pressure. Batsmen of the calibre of Richards and Gavaskar can change gear at any time.

Whilst fielding at first slip to Botham you share all these concerns with Paul Downton, who does his best to reassure you that the breakthrough will come if we 'keep plugging away'. However, even the optimistic keeper admits that 'we could do with a wicket now before Richards really gets going'. You agree. 61-1 from eighteen overs.

Turn to page 105

During Emburey's next over Richards decides to break the stalemate, nonchalantly flicking the off-spinner over square leg and then stepping away to cut him towards Old Father Time. This prompts you to tell Neil Foster to be ready to bowl the next over from the Pavilion End. Botham's next over brings just a single to Gavaskar making the score 70-1 from 20 overs. In the commentary box Ray Illingworth is gloomy; the Rest of the World have had an excellent start and 'England are going to have to work hard to get back into this game'. In the middle you sense that the fieldsmen are no longer 'razor-sharp' and there's a slight air of resignation. You clap your hands vigorously but you're not sure whether that makes any difference. A chimpanzee can clap his hands vigorously but there are very few of them captaining cricket teams. You are desperate for a wicket though you do your best to hide this desperation from your team-mates.

Foster now starts a new spell from the Pavilion End; as he delivers his first ball you see Umpire Bird's arm outstretched and you hear the muffled cry of 'No-ball'. Gavaskar clips the ball off his legs in the air straight to Bill Athey at mid-wicket, who completes the catch albeit off a no-ball. Disappointment now turns to confusion when you notice that Gavaskar is slowly making his way towards the pavilion, presumably thinking that he's out. By now Downton, conscientious keeper that he is, has made his way up to the stumps. Bill Athey is looking to you for directions. Suddenly you realise that there is a possibility of running Gavaskar out. You must make an immediate decision.

A. Do you motion to Bill Athey to lob the ball to Downton so that Gavaskar can be dismissed? Or

B. Do you instruct him to hold on to the ball whilst you call Gavaskar back?

If **A** turn to page 106
If **B** turn to page 109

A. You motion to Athey to throw the ball to Downton.

'Take 'em off, Paul,' you yell from first slip. Downton obeys. Gavaskar suddenly realises his mistake and stops dead in the middle of the wicket. Beneath his wide-brimmed floppy hat he remains outwardly imperturbable. You wonder whether inside he is fuming or quietly resigned to going back to the pavilion as a result of a freak dismissal. It occurs to you that cricket at the top is a tough profession. It hasn't taken you long to realise that and act upon it. Gavaskar, of all people, having scored more Test runs than any other cricketer in history, must be aware that this is a ruthless game.

The little Indian remains motionless in the middle of the wicket. Is he still too stunned by the episode to leave the field? You decide it's time he departed and turning to David Shepherd at square leg you shout, 'Owzat, umpire'.

In his best Devonian accent a red-faced David Shepherd bellows back: 'That's not out.'

Gavaskar calmly returns to his crease and awaits the next ball. You are feeling rather more animated and you sprint over to the square-leg umpire with images of Shakoor Rana and Mike Gatting racing through your head. You are reasonably restrained upon arrival: 'What's going on? He was miles out of his crease.'

David Shepherd remains calm, 'I realise that but don't you know the laws of the game? If my memory serves me correctly it is Law 38 section 2 which states that "If a no-ball has been called, the striker shall not be given run out unless he attempts to run." Sunil was not attempting a run so he's not out. Shall we get on with the game now?'

To say that you are crestfallen is an understatement. Not only is Gavaskar still in, but you have made a complete fool of yourself in front of a capacity crowd, millions of TV viewers and, most importantly, your new team-mates. 71-1 in the 21st over.

Turn to page 110

Sunil Gavaskar recovers his concentration after the 'incident'

B. Whilst the ball is still swirling in the air you quickly try to assess which of the two fielders is best placed to take the catch since it is clear that neither is aware of the other's presence. You decide that Gooch is your man since he is moving to his right and you yell 'Graham' at the top of your voice. The moment you have closed your mouth you recognise your mistake. Having heard the call both players move towards the ball with renewed urgency, their eyes fixed intently upon its flight path. As the ball reaches the end of its descent England's opening batsman collides unceremoniously with England's opening bowler and they end up in an undignified heap in front of the press box. The cameras of Messrs Eagar and Murrell click furiously. Neither Graham touches the ball, which trickles innocently over the boundary rope. The only consolation is that Gooch and Dilley avoid injury, but once they have untangled themselves they both glare meaningfully in your direction. One or two of your colleagues can't avoid a surreptitious giggle but you can't quite bring yourself to join in, neither can Botham.

Now after such a tragicomedy of errors you are even more desperate for a wicket and you decide to shuffle the bowlers around, bringing back Foster at the Pavilion End and introducing Edmonds, who by now is anxious to enter the action, at the Nursery End. Botham appears somewhat reluctant to take his sweater after nearly dismissing Richards but you decide that it is vital to assert your authority especially since everything seems to be going awry. You are beginning to look forward to a cup of tea and a chance to assess the situation calmly.

Edmonds and Foster both bowl accurately but no breakthrough is forthcoming. Richards decides to take no more risks and 'plays for tea' and Gavaskar just keeps ticking over methodically. So you are not a happy person as you return to the pavilion with the score at 90-1 after 25 overs. To make matters worse Foster is complaining of a sore hamstring.

Turn to page 112

B. You shout over to Gavaskar: 'Sunil, it's OK; come on back.' The little Indian is clearly a little surprised by the turn of events; he smiles graciously and calmly retraces his steps. However, a few of your colleagues are less content with the outcome and you can't help overhearing a few comments like 'What does he think this is – a benefit match?' and 'Do we want to win this game or not?'

When the furore dies down you explain to all the players who gather around you in the middle: 'Even if we had taken the bails off he would not have been out. Aren't you aware of the run-out law – Law 38 section 2 I think it is – "When a no-ball has been called, the striker shall not be given out unless he's attempting to run"? That's right, isn't it?'

'You're absolutely right there, captain. Not many people, apart from us Umpires, are aware of that law,' replies Umpire Dickie Bird.

'Right lads, let's keep it tight now.'

Your players disperse swiftly to their positions; there's no doubt that they are impressed by your handling of the situation as well as your knowledge of the laws. Their confidence in you rises a little especially when you pull off a fine diving stop when Gavaskar edges Foster's next delivery. Now you decide that it is time to bring on Edmonds from the Nursery End. He's been eager to enter the action for a while now, particularly since his contribution with the bat had hardly been decisive. After lengthy consultations a field is agreed and you're relieved when all the elaborate and detailed manoeuvres of the nine available fielders results in a maiden over despite some powerful drives by Richards. At the other end Foster maintains the pressure and in the penultimate over before tea Richards advances down the wicket to the left-arm spinner; the ball turns past the outside edge of his bat and Downton jubilantly removes the bails so that the team is cock-a-hoop when they return to the pavilion at tea with the score at 80-2 from 25 overs. Gavaskar has 29. Martin Crowe has one.

Turn to page 115

Up in the commentary box Fred Trueman holds his hand over the microphone and asks the assembled throng: 'What's going on out there?' Producer Peter Baxter finds the laws and quickly explains, whereupon Fred does the same to his audience.

Meanwhile down in the middle Gavaskar, his concentration disturbed by the incident, edges the next ball to you at first slip. You fail to lay a hand on the ball which goes through your legs to the boundary. You feel considerably less than six feet tall and stare at your bootlaces for a while. Things are not going according to plan. Downton, ever cheerful, says 'Come on, stick at it, skip,' before encouraging the rest of the team at full volume, whilst you make a mental note never to condemn Mike Gatting again in your local pub at home.

By now you are becoming desperate for a wicket. You decide that it's time to introduce Edmonds at the Nursery End. He is clearly anxious to get into the game particularly since his contribution with the bat was scarcely earth shattering. He is meticulous in his field placements moving his men a yard to the left here, a fraction deeper there. You wonder whether he isn't overdoing it especially since slow over-rates can result in heavy fines. You think about hurrying him up but your confidence is currently at such a low ebb that you let him do whatever he likes.

Edmonds soon finds his rhythm but is unable to provide that much-needed breakthrough as both batsmen sedately 'play for tea'. They can afford to play quietly for a couple of overs since they've maintained a run-rate of nearly four an over throughout the innings.

So you are not a happy person when Dickie Bird announces that it's time for tea. The Rest of the World's score has advanced to 90-1 from 25 overs and, to make matters worse, as you're leaving the field Neil Foster tells you that his right hamstring is feeling sore.

Turn to page 112

A. As the ball swirls in the air you stifle your call of 'Graham' just in time. That wouldn't have clarified anything since both fieldsmen answer to that name. So you rely upon their good sense and sure enough Graham – Gooch, that is – calls 'Mine' decisively. Dilley decelerates, no doubt breathing a sigh of relief at the same time, and makes sure that he stays out of Gooch's way. The Essex opener continues running and completes an excellent catch and then hurls the ball up into the heavens in an uncharacteristic display of emotion. Botham is equally jubilant and rushes over to congratulate Gooch; indeed the dismissal of Richards gives everyone fresh hope.

Martin Crowe replaces Vivian Richards.

Botham greets his former colleague with a bouncer and Crowe sways out of the way easily, almost as if he had been expecting it. Thereafter Botham maintains a disciplined line on off stump and since Crowe is disinclined to take any risks with tea approaching the run-rate slows dramatically. For the first time in the innings the English bowlers begin to exert some pressure on the opposition batsmen. In an effort to sneak another wicket before tea you opt to switch your bowlers around, bringing back Foster at the Pavilion End and introducing Phil Edmonds, who by now is impatient to get into the game, at the Nursery End. Edmonds is meticulous about his field placements and it seems to take all of five minutes to satisfy his exact requirements. You wonder briefly about that fine for slow over-rates but decide not to say anything since it is far more important that he should be happy with his field. Trevor Bailey deplores the hold-up whilst Henry Blofeld spots some pigeons to talk about. However, the delay seems justified when he begins with a maiden to Martin Crowe. With Gavaskar scoring only in singles and Crowe temporarily becalmed the score has only progressed to 80-2 from 25 overs when Dickie Bird announces that it's time for a cup of tea. You leave the field relatively content with the situation.

Turn to page 115

You are grateful for twenty minutes respite. In the dressing room the tea is already poured along with several glasses of squash and there are plenty of sandwiches available. Most of them are left untouched since this is not the time to fill your stomach. Now you have a chance to consider the state of the game and, at the moment, it is clear that the Rest of the World are on course to win. They need another 175 runs from 35 overs, still a taxing target but Richards is in ominously good form and Gavaskar hasn't really tried to open out yet. In addition, Foster and the physiotherapist come over to tell you that his hamstring is slightly torn and there is no guarantee that he will be able to complete his overs. After several minutes' discussion you decide that Foster should try to complete his quota of overs straight after tea in harness with Edmonds who has so far been economical, though not especially threatening. Sooner than expected the five-minute bell clangs. You remind the players of India's famous World Cup victory against the West Indies in 1983 in the hope that the memory may spark a similar occurrence and set off again for the middle.

In the first over after tea your problems compound. Gavaskar drives Edmonds firmly to extra cover, where Gooch makes a spectacular stop but in doing so splits the webbing in his left hand. He leaves the field immediately for repairs and a young member of the Lord's ground staff comes out to replace him. Edmonds completes a maiden over leaving Foster to resume his spell bowling to Richards.

Foster runs up to the wicket gingerly, but bowls a no ball. Richards straight-drives and Foster instinctively lunges to his right in an attempt to stop the ball. He manages to get his right foot to it but then collapses in agony on the pitch. Now his hamstring is well and truly torn and it is clear that he will take no further part in the game. Perhaps the decision to bowl him again was irresponsible but, as he's carried from the field, you cannot allow this to be your prime concern. Someone has to complete his over and the most obvious choice, Graham Gooch, is not on the pitch. You are a bowler short. A swift decision is required and you stun your colleagues by shouting: 'OK, give me the ball. I'm bowling.' Downton trots up the pitch and asks politely where he should stand. You tell him. You signal your bemused colleagues into position, electing not to have any close catchers since Richards is obviously in fine form and you mark out your normal run-up. The crowd is hushed and curious, so are your team-mates; only Richards seems relaxed.

Your first ball is a disappointment. It is a high full toss. The only consolation is that it is so unusually bad that Richards opts to play it back down the pitch. Five balls remain in the over and you spot one or two of the fielders glancing anxiously at one another. Your second delivery is much better; it is straight and a good length. Again Richards pats it back and Downton and Botham bellow 'Well bowled'. Your confidence rises. Perhaps this bowling change will prove to be your master-stroke. The next ball is again straight and well pitched but this time Richards moves his left foot outside the line and cracks the ball like a bullet to the square-leg boundary. For the first time you feel the exasperation that bowlers around the world have experienced for the last decade. As the fourth ball leaves your hand you are quite pleased. It is a little faster than its predecessors and again it is straight. Richards swings it effortlessly to the mid-wicket boundary. There are now two balls left and it occurs to you that the match will be irretrievable if Richards keeps hitting you for four. Emburey suggests that you move another fielder to the leg-side boundary and bowl outside leg stump, at least reducing the likelihood of being hit for four. Gower advocates bowling a little slower but still aiming for the stumps. Somehow you have to get rid of two more balls without throwing away the game. Do you take the advice of

A. Emburey? Or
B. Gower?

If **A** turn to page 117
If **B** turn to page 114

B. You run up and bowl a slower ball on middle stump. Richards moves across to the off side and with a casual flick of the wrist times the ball to perfection. You wince until you see Gower take off to his left and pluck the ball out of the air one-handed. It takes a moment to sink in but, when you realise that Richards is slowly dragging himself towards the pavilion, you cannot restrain yourself from completing a jig of delight as if you had scored a goal in a Wembley Cup final. You charge over to mid-wicket fully intending to embrace the former England captain, who senses your intentions. He is clearly none too keen on the idea and contrives to hide behind Botham until your passion abates. Indeed by way of contrast Gower merely permits himself a sheepish grin whilst observing that his catch was 'a bit of a bonus'.

On TV Richie Benaud is saying things like 'You wouldn't dare write this in a piece of fiction' whilst in the Radio 3 commentary box someone observes that cricket is a funny game; Trevor Bailey adds that the England captain has bowled 'very sensibly'.

Meanwhile Martin Crowe is making his way to the middle accompanied by Graham Gooch, whose left hand has been carefully strapped by the physiotherapist. He tells you that he's fine and perfectly capable of bowling if required; Foster, however, will take no further part in the game. There is one ball left in the over; it is not one of your better ones, short and wide of off stump. Crowe hits it sweetly but it goes straight to extra cover. You have bowling figures of 1-0-8-1 and the crowd applaud enthusiastically.

Edmonds's next over yields just one run, bringing up the hundred for the Rest of the World from 28 overs. There are three overs still required from a non-specialist bowler; the question is do you

A. bring on Gooch, your obvious sixth bowler? Or

B. given your recent, spectacular success, elect to bowl another one yourself?

If **A** turn to page 116
If **B** turn to page 118

Back in the dressing room the tea is already poured along with several glasses of squash; there are also plenty of sandwiches, most of which will remain untouched and Botham suggests that the bulk of them be wrapped up and saved for after the game. You have more important things on your mind. As you sip your tea, you consider the state of the game. The dismissal of Richards just before tea means that the game is back on an even keel, a view duplicated by Ray Illingworth on the TV before someone urges that the volume be turned down. As you are pondering your strategy Neil Foster comes over to tell you that he has a slightly torn hamstring and is unlikely to be able to bowl again in the innings. After several minutes of discussion you decide that Foster should stay off the field and that your sixth bowler, Gooch, should replace him immediately at the Pavilion End with Edmonds continuing at the Nursery End.

Sooner than expected the five-minute bell clangs and after a few forgettable words of encouragement you lead England out on to the field for the final and decisive session of play. After tea the batsmen begin confidently, Crowe using his feet to drive Edmonds to the extra-cover boundary and Gavaskar straight-driving Gooch to the pavilion steps. However, your two experienced bowlers maintain their concentration and by the 31st over with the score on 105-2 the batsmen have been reduced to picking up their runs in singles. Walking in at extra cover as Gooch approaches to bowl to Gavaskar you feel in control of affairs. Gavaskar drives the ball firmly to your left; you dive, stop the ball and end up facing the boundary rather than the wicket. Whilst making the stop you hear the call of 'Yes' followed sharply by a more desperate 'No'. Now you hear the excited shouts of your team-mates: 'This end'; 'That end'. With the ball now in your throwing hand you realise that there has been a misunderstanding between the batsmen. You must decide immediately which end to throw the ball. Do you choose
A. the wicket-keeper's end? Or
B. the bowler's end?

If **A** turn to page 120
If **B** turn to page 119

A. It is sorely tempting to have another over, but your reasoning is sound. Gooch is a proven bowler in this type of cricket; you are not. What's more lightning rarely strikes twice. Your decision seems to be vindicated when Gooch concedes just one run in his first over. The spectators, pundits and players are all impressed. To have the confidence to bowl yourself, take the vital wicket and then to withdraw yourself immediately from the attack displays the sort of flair – and good fortune – that the selectors were looking for when they transported you from the happy obscurity of your local side.

At the other end Edmonds continues to bowl tightly, preventing the batsmen from hitting boundaries. Indeed Crowe and Gavaskar are reduced to scrambling for singles just like ordinary mortals. The gloom of the tea interval has now given way to a fresh optimism. You feel in control of the game, where the fielders should stand and which bowlers to use, and it's a wonderful feeling, one that has eluded you up until now.

At the beginning of the 31st over the score is 105-2 and Gooch is about to bowl to Gavaskar. From your position of extra cover you move Lamb a little squarer on the leg-side boundary and then dutifully walk in as the bowler approaches the wicket.

Gavaskar drives the ball firmly to your left; you dive, stop the ball and end up facing the boundary rather than the wicket. Whilst making the stop you hear the call of 'Yes' followed sharply by a more desperate 'No'. Now you hear the excited shouts of your team-mates: 'This end'; 'That end'. With the ball now in your throwing hand you realise that there has been a misunderstanding between the batsmen, even though you haven't actually been able to witness it. You must decide immediately which end to throw the ball. Do you choose

A. the wicket-keeper's end? Or

B. the bowler's end?

If **A** turn to page 120

If **B** turn to page 119

A. The leg-side field is reinforced and the next two deliveries duly yield two more singles. At the end of the over you feel relieved, particularly when you see Graham Gooch, his left hand neatly bandaged trotting on to the field. Immediately you inform him that he will be bowling the next over at the Pavilion End.

In Edmonds's next over Richards steps outside leg stump and crashes the ball over extra cover; your one over seems to have removed any of the restraints he might have placed on himself. To the next ball Richards advances down the wicket; Edmonds doesn't actually see him coming; rather he feels him coming and he pitches the ball shorter; even better it turns past the outside edge of Richards's bat leaving Downton with the relatively simple task of removing the bails. Edmonds is jubilant; so are you since England are back in the game; another half hour of Richards and it would have been all over.

Martin Crowe replaces Vivian Richards.

Gooch bowls three overs, thereby completing Foster's quota; they are tidy but unthreatening and Gavaskar and Crowe, who swiftly finds his touch, maintain the required momentum. Gavaskar reaches his half century, a compact, undemonstrative innings – a delight to the purist – and this prompts you to ask Dilley to bowl a short spell from the Pavilion End. It's a happy choice since in his second over Dilley produces the perfect away-swinger, which Gavaskar snicks to the ever-grateful Downton. 136-3 in the 37th over. Out strides Allan Border, looking typically purposeful. It would certainly help your cause if you could get rid of him early. It occurs to you that it might be a good idea if Dilley bounced him first ball before his eye is in. As he takes guard you are still talking to your opening bowler; you can recall how uncomfortable Border made you feel at the beginning of your innings. Do you

A. instruct Dilley to bowl a bouncer? Or

B. tell him to keep bowling a line and length?

If **A** turn to page 126
If **B** turn to page 123

B. You opt to bowl another one yourself; after all, if Richards can be persuaded to succumb to you, why shouldn't Gavaskar or Crowe? Such an argument seems perfectly reasonable at the beginning of the over, but less convincing after six balls. With ruthless efficiency the batsmen help themselves to a four and two singles each; like two children sharing a bar of chocolate, neither wanted to be seen to take more than his fair share. Clearly lightning was not going to strike twice today; you now instruct Gooch to get loose, wishing you had done so two overs earlier. Bill Frindall passes a note to Christopher Martin-Jenkins who informs millions of listeners that your bowling figures are now 2-0-20-1.

Gooch now bowls two overs rather more economically, but he doesn't worry the batsmen unduly as they maintain the momentum of the innings. At least there is no longer the necessity to use a sixth bowler again.

Gavaskar cuts Edmonds down to the Tavern to reach his fifty and the Lord's crowd, conscious that they may never see the little man batting again, give him a generous round of applause.

A change in the attack is clearly needed and you decide upon a short burst from Graham Dilley at the Pavilion End. This proves to be a happy choice since he produces a perfect away-swinger in his second over, which the Indian can only edge to the wicket-keeper. Downton gratefully receives the catch. 136-3 in the 37th over.

Gavaskar is replaced by captain Allan Border. As you are talking to your fast bowler you remember the pressure that the Australian had applied when you came to the crease. You are anxious to retaliate somehow; extra close fielders are out of the question at this stage of the game but it occurs to you that it might be a good idea to instruct Dilley to bounce him first ball before his eye is in. As Border takes guard do you

A. instruct Dilley to bowl a bouncer? Or

B. encourage him to bowl his usual length ball?

If **A** turn to page 126
If **B** turn to page 123

B. You hurl the ball at the stumps at the bowler's end with all your might and to your delight achieve a direct hit. However your euphoria is soon dampened when you spot that both Gavaskar and Crowe have made their ground at the bowler's end whilst twenty-two yards away Paul Downton is feeling distinctly lonely. To make matters worse the ball ricochets off the stumps down to the pavilion steps so that the only decision that Dickie Bird is required to make is whether the batting side is entitled to four or five runs. After a moment's thought he opts for four since amidst the pandemonium it is debatable whether the batsmen actually crossed, Gavaskar having finally retreated back to the striker's end. Thus, arguably the best piece of fielding of your career ends with the concession of four runs. This episode seems to prompt Gavaskar to be more aggressive; perhaps this is his lucky day. In Edmonds's next over he makes room to square-cut and the ball races down to the Tavern for four: an on-drive off Gooch takes him past the fifty mark. With Crowe also playing with greater freedom your problems mount. Clearly a change is required and you decide to give Graham Dilley a short burst from the Pavilion End; it is vital that this partnership is broken soon.

The recall of Dilley is a success. In his second over he produces the perfect away-swinger, which Gavaskar succeeds only in edging to the wicket-keeper, who gratefully accepts a straightforward catch. 136-3 in the 37th over. You run over to congratulate Dilley and your opposite number Allan Border strides purposefully to the wicket. You recall the intense pressure that Border himself created when you first arrived at the crease four hours ago and you are especially anxious to give him the same treatment. However, at this stage of the game extra close catchers are out of the question, but it occurs to you that this might be a good time to instruct Dilley to bowl a bouncer – before Border's eye is in. So do you

A. tell Dilley to bowl a bouncer? Or

B. tell him to bowl his normal length?

If **A** turn to page 126
If **B** turn to page 123

A. The ball arrives straight into the gloves of Paul Downton, who immediately removes the bails. However, he doesn't bother to appeal; it really isn't necessary since Gavaskar is left stranded halfway down the wicket. The little Indian quietly accepts his fate and receives a warm reception from the crowd. Your colleagues rush around you full of congratulations, whilst you attempt – unsuccessfully – to give the impression that such a piece of fielding was nothing out of the ordinary for you.

Your euphoria is dented a little when Ian Botham trots over to tell you that his back is giving him pain and you agree to his going off for treatment. He assures you that he will be back in time to complete his spell. So as Border arrives on to the playing area his former Queensland colleague leaves it. A glance at the new clock next to the Mound Stand tells you that it's 5.30; in about two hours time it will all be over, but no one can predict the winner at this stage.

Border is quickly into his stride cover-driving Gooch to the boundary. You decide to bring back Dilley for a short burst from the Pavilion End. Crowe is also starting to dominate, using his feet against Edmonds who has now bowled eight overs in succession; clearly the batsmen are getting used to him. At five to six Botham returns and announces that he's fit to bowl, which is a relief. Two injuries to your main bowlers would be too much to bear.

You decide that it is time for a change of bowling at the Nursery End. Edmonds has bowled excellently but it might be better if his last few overs could be bowled to a new batsman. However your choices are limited with Foster off the field. As Dilley completes the 37th over with the score 129-3, you must decide who you want to replace Edmonds. Should you choose
A. Botham? Or
B. Emburey?

If **A** turn to page 122
If **B** turn to page 124

A formality for Downton

A. You decide that three overs of Botham is the best bet and you summon him to the Nursery End. Upon hearing your call he looks strangely hesitant. Of any professional cricketer currently playing the game you had imagined that he most enjoyed being in the thick of the action and for a moment his apparent reluctance to bowl puzzles you. You begin discussing field placements with him. Once your plan of campaign has become clear to all you are surprised to see the rotund figure of David Shepherd ambling towards you.

'Ian can't bowl.'

'I don't see that the merit of my bowlers has anything to do with you, Mr Shepherd,' you reply trying not to sound too pompous.

'That's not the point,' says Shepherd as amicably as possible. 'He's been off the field for more than a quarter of an hour – 24 minutes to be precise – which means he can't bowl again until 6.18; that's in twenty minutes time.' As unobtrusively as possible you shout to John Emburey on the square-cover boundary and tell him to have a bowl, whilst your error is explained to millions of listeners and viewers around the country. One or two of your players are unable to stifle a grin; however, deep down they are concerned by such a gaffe, even though it isn't costly in terms of runs conceded. None the less the introduction of Emburey brings a swift reward. Crowe comes down the wicket once again but this time Emburey spots him and he fizzes the ball down the leg-side for Downton to complete an excellent stumping. Botham observes that it was a good job he went off for treatment.

Imran comes to the wicket and plays himself in carefully, whilst Border is now batting fluently, once hitting Emburey over the sightscreen. At 6.18 precisely you bring on Botham at the Pavilion End in place of Dilley and after a three-over spell from Emburey you decide to bring back Edmonds to bowl his final overs since the off-spinner is better suited to bowling near the end of the innings. 161-4 from 43 overs.

Turn to page 125

B. Dilley keeps his line and length and Border struggles to find his touch. The Australian captain is too experienced a campaigner to worry unduly about his slow start; none the less he yearns for something to cut or pull. Dilley refuses to oblige.

At the other end Emburey replaces Edmonds. The left-arm spinner has bowled eight overs on the trot and Martin Crowe is just beginning to dominate against him so it seems sensible to change the line of attack. The New Zealander adopts his usual policy against the off-spinner, coming down the wicket almost every ball in an attempt to disrupt his length. This makes it easier for him to hit the ball on the half-volley usually driving it to long-on or deep mid-wicket for comfortable singles. Emburey tries to combat this ploy by bowling a quicker ball down the leg side. Wicket-keeper Paul Downton anticipates this delivery rather better than Crowe (this is hardly surprising since he had been forewarned) and he deftly removes the bails leaving Crowe stranded down the wicket. The Middlesex pair are delighted by their collaboration since such a plan succeeds about once in every fifty attempts.

The princely Imran replaces Crowe and, whilst he is playing himself in, it is left to Border to seize the initiative, which he does pulling Dilley viciously to the mid-wicket boundary and then lofting Emburey over the sightscreen.

You decide to keep juggling your bowlers around bringing Botham on for Dilley and after just three overs from Emburey you recall Edmonds at the Nursery End. There are several good reasons for this. You know that Edmonds particularly relishes duels with Border; by his own admission they bring the best out of him. Also you want to have a few Emburey overs up your sleeve for the later stages of the innings; he is more suited to bowling then than Edmonds. So with the score standing at 161-4 from 43 overs Edmonds tosses his sweater to David Shepherd and prepares to bowl to Allan Border.

Please turn to page 125

B. Against Emburey, Martin Crowe comes down the wicket to almost every ball. This enables him to get to the pitch of the ball and to drive it on the half-volley usually to long-on or deep mid-wicket for a comfortable single. Now Emburey takes a calculated risk and opts to fizz the ball as quickly as possible down the leg side. Downton who has been alerted to the plan is waiting for it and neatly whips off the bails with Crowe stranded down the wicket. This is the most satisfying of dismissals for the Middlesex pair since the normal success-rate for such a ploy is no more than 1 in 50. As he sets off for the pavilion Crowe quietly acknowledges their expertise.

The princely Imran now enters and plays himself in carefully; however, his caution doesn't affect the run-rate adversely because Border is now in vintage form, once hitting the off-spinner over the sightscreen and cutting and pulling Dilley viciously. At 6.20 you bring on Botham in place of Dilley at the Pavilion End. You would have preferred to bowl him earlier but you realise that after his 25-minute break for treatment this is the earliest you can recall him into the attack.

After Emburey's third over you tell him to have a break and you signal to Edmonds to take over. Of the two Middlesex spinners Emburey is the more adept at bowling towards the end of the innings so you want to keep a few of his overs up your sleeve. You also know that Edmonds has an excellent record against Border and that the duel with the Australian captain excites him. By his own admission he's far more likely to bowl well against a batsman of Border's calibre than against his Australian colleague, Bruce Reid, whose batting skills may be euphemistically described as limited.

So with four overs left in his quota Edmonds rubs his hand in the bowling creases so that he can grip the ball better and tosses his bulky sweater to David Shepherd. The score is 161-4 after 43 overs.

Please turn to page 125

Border responds immediately by advancing down the wicket and driving him into the Mound Stand; next he leans back and square-cuts him for four. Edmonds is clearly annoyed and you begin to wonder about the wisdom of your decision as eleven runs accrue from the over. At the beginning of his next over Imran is on strike; the Pakistani sensing Edmonds's unrest decides to join the assault but ends up slicing the ball to long-off where Emburey completes a fine catch. 176-5 and Dujon comes to the wicket. Edmonds is only mildly cheered by his success; he's still smarting after those blows from his arch adversary Border.

As Dujon takes guard the left-arm spinner waves his arms to the vast majority of the fieldsmen moving them here and there a yard at a time. The whole process takes an age and you are conscious that a hefty fine will result unless the over-rate picks up. You enter the action by signalling Emburey up from long-off to orthodox mid-off. You reason that Border is in such devastating form that he must be kept from the strike and Dujon should not be allowed a single from a gentle off-drive. Edmonds waves Emburey back to the boundary.

Now you go up to Edmonds and explain your reasoning. He replies that he wants Dujon to try to push the ball to long-off; there's a good chance of a caught and bowled if he does. He also questions whether you regard yourself as a better judge of the correct field placements for a left-arm spinner than he is and as if terminating the conversation he shouts: 'Stay back there, Embers.'

By now Emburey is in no man's land, unsure which way to turn. He looks towards you for guidance. Umpire David Shepherd is urging you to get on with the game 'or the pubs will be shut'. The score is 176-5 after 43 overs. Do you

A. accede to Edmonds's wishes and signal Emburey to the boundary? Or

B. bring Emburey up to mid-off and continue the argument with your left-arm spinner?

If **A** turn to page 132
If **B** turn to page 127

A. It is a bold decision to bounce Border first ball since it is acknowledged that he is one of the best players of the pull and hook shot in the world. None the less it sometimes pays to bowl to a player's strength early in his innings; he may be tempted to play his favourite shot before he has adjusted to the pace and bounce of the wicket, with fatal consequences.

On this occasion Dilley produces an excellent bouncer directed at off stump and rising steeply. Border moves on to the back foot and prepares to play the ball defensively; however he is surprised by the bounce and at the last minute he withdraws his left hand from the bat as he takes evasive action. The ball clips his left glove and as a result loses much of its momentum. Behind the stumps Downton dives forward at full stretch and claims the catch. At first slip Botham leaps in the air appealing vociferously.

'Not out' bellows Umpire Bird.

Now Botham shouts over to the square-leg umpire: 'Did that carry, Shep?'

'Yes, the ball did carry.'

You are still at mid-off and you feel a growing pressure from your team-mates to intervene in some way. Some of them are showing obvious signs of astonishment at Umpire Bird's decision. As for yourself you are reluctant to enter into any argument with the umpire. The events in Pakistan in the winter of 1987 are still fresh in your mind and the last thing you want is to be embroiled in an umpiring controversy on your debut. However it is clear that you must do something. The score in the thirty-seventh over is 136-3. Do you

A. tell your players to get into position for the next ball, whilst congratulating Dilley on his last delivery? Or

B. go up to Dickie Bird and politely inform him that his colleague has confirmed that the ball carried to the wicket-keeper?

If **A** turn to page 130
If **B** turn to page 129

B. 'Phil, I want Embers at orthodox mid-off, please. If you don't like it I'll find someone else to bowl.' The seconds tick away as Edmonds considers his response; your players await it with intense interest. So do you.

In the commentary box Brian Johnston observes that 'there is a long discussion between the England captain and his left-arm spinner over field placements'. The tabloid journalists in the press box are interpreting the episode rather differently. They can sense a story along the lines of 'Edmonds snubs new skipper', which will delight their hungry sports editors. Everyone watches intently.

Finally Edmonds shrugs his shoulders, moves silently back to his mark and prepares to bowl to Dujon. The West Indian drives his first ball straight to Emburey at mid-off and there is no run. Despite the disagreement Edmonds bowls with superb control and variation and keeps Dujon tied down. The final ball of the over is tossed a little higher; Dujon anxious to get off the mark drives freely; the ball skims to mid-off; Emburey leaps into the air and completes a brilliant catch. You are jubilant; having applauded Emburey, you join Edmonds at the bowler's end. He's smiling. He pats you on the back and acknowledges that events have proved you right. You heave a sigh of relief, thankful that Dujon's drive had not finished up on the long-off boundary. The score is now 176-6 after 44 overs as Roger Harper makes his way to the middle.

With just four wickets remaining, Border is compelled to exercise a little more caution whilst Harper plays himself in. They progress mostly through singles, Harper's giant strides providing a comic contrast to Border's quick scurrying steps. Edmonds, in harness with Botham, maintains the pressure and is applauded by players and spectators alike when he completes his twelve overs in the fiftieth over of the innings. The score is 199-6. Anybody's game.

Please turn to page 135

John Emburerey runs in to bowl under the watchful gaze of umpire David Shepherd

B. You try to be as tactful as possible.

'Dickie, David Shepherd at square leg thinks that the ball carried to the keeper.'

'I knew it did, skipper.'

'Then why haven't you given him out?'

Umpire Bird adjusts his sleeves nervously and a wide grin spreads across his face: 'Because when the ball struck Border's glove, his left hand was not holding the bat. He had removed it from the handle. In those circumstances you cannot be given out caught. It's all there in Law 32 if you want to check it.' You don't want to check it. You just wish you had kept quiet. The incident excites the press box for a while but Dickie Bird's patient response to your query ensures that it does not reach Faisalabad proportions. The tabloids must find another headline. Now you decide to try Emburey at the Nursery End in place of Edmonds and you are heartened when it appears that you've done something right. Crowe comes down the wicket to the off-spinner, who fires the ball down the leg-side: Crowe is stranded and Downton executes a superb stumping.

Imran Khan takes his time to settle but this doesn't affect the run-rate too much because Border now seizes the initiative. He pulls another bouncer from Dilley to the mid-wicket boundary and then hits a perfectly respectable off-spinner from Emburey over the sightscreen. In an attempt to upset Border's rhythm you juggle your bowlers around, replacing Dilley with Botham, and after just three overs from Emburey at the Nursery End you bring back Edmonds who relishes the challenge of bowling to Australia's captain. Border is unperturbed by the changes but they seem to unsettle Imran who skies a slower ball from Edmonds to extra cover. 176-5 and Dujon ambles casually to the wicket and gets off the mark first ball. After an over from Botham the score stands at 183-5 from 45 overs and Christopher Martin-Jenkins observes that 'we're in for a splendid finish'.

Turn to page 133

A. Some of the players are still bemused by the decision and disappointed by your apparent reluctance to take the matter up with Dickie Bird. Now you explain to them that from your vantage point at mid-off it was obvious that the ball had flicked Border's glove, but it was also clear that his left hand was no longer holding the bat when contact was made. Therefore it was irrelevant whether Downton had made a clean catch since a batsman cannot be given out caught off the glove if his hand isn't on the bat. Once this is explained the players concerned readily acknowledge their mistake and the game resumes without rancour. The Secretary of the TCCB, who has had his fill of umpiring controversies recently, breathes a sigh of relief.

By now Martin Crowe is beginning to look dangerous particularly when facing the bowling of Edmonds so you decide to bring on Emburey. The change pays dividends when Crowe is stumped by a clever piece of bowling by the England off-spinner. Seeing Crowe advancing down the wicket he fires the ball quickly down the leg-side and Downton executes a superlative stumping. Crowe is replaced by Imran Khan, who plays sedately whilst Border seizes the initiative pulling a less effective bouncer from Dilley to the mid-wicket boundary and, soon after, lofting Emburey over the sightscreen. Now you decide to juggle your bowlers around in an effort to unsettle Border, who looks in ominously good form. Botham takes over from Dilley at the Pavilion End and after just three overs from Emburey you recall Edmonds, who always enjoys the challenge of bowling to the Australian captain. These changes don't appear to upset Border in the slightest but Edmonds does manage to deceive Imran who miscues a drive and is caught at extra cover making the score 176-5 in the forty-fourth over. Jeffrey Dujon ambles casually to the wicket and drives Edmonds to long-off to get off the mark and when Botham completes his next over the score stands at 183-5 from 45 overs. Illingworth on TV observes that 'this will be a good game to win'.

Turn to page 133

Crowe on the attack

A. Finally and with a touch of irritation you wave your arms at Emburey, signalling him back to the boundary's edge at long-off. Dujon, who has been waiting most patiently, settles into his stance and awaits his first ball. He drives at it casually and the ball skims through the air to mid-off or – to be more precise – where mid-off would have been if you had chosen to have one. The West Indian jogs down the wicket with a quiet smile on his face, almost as if he had played the shot on purpose to rub salt into your wound. Edmonds assures you that he wouldn't have played that shot if Emburey had been up in the ring. You are not entirely convinced by this but the question is now an academic one.

None the less you are annoyed with yourself for giving in to Edmonds's wishes and you make a mental note to follow your own instincts in future. You may not have a wealth of first-class experience behind you, but there's no point you being out there as captain if you are going to yield to everyone else's wishes. Captaincy by committee has rarely proved successful for any cricket team.

Four balls remain in the over. Border and Edmonds continue their private battle. When Edmonds senses the left-hander advancing down the wicket, he drops the ball shorter forcing the Australian to play defensively. Then Border feints to come down the wicket, hoping to induce Edmonds to pitch short so that he can play his favourite pull shot. But Edmonds is not deceived. On the last ball of the over Border advances down the wicket again and even though he fails to reach the pitch of the ball, he follows through swinging with the spin and the ball sails into the Mound Stand. Maybe a moral victory to Edmonds, but it's six runs to Border. So ends an eventful over.

You are relieved that Botham bowls a timely maiden over at the Pavilion End to Dujon, who is still feeling his way. After 45 overs the score is 183-5 and Richie Benaud observes that 'we've got an excellent game of cricket on our hands here today'.

Turn to page 133

It is imperative that you apply as much pressure as you can on the new batsman, Dujon, so you bring an extra man into the ring when he is on strike and you urge your fielders to save the single. However, when Border is facing, the field is more deeply set as you are more concerned to prevent him hitting any boundaries. For a while this system works well, with Border taking singles almost at will, but Dujon struggling to break the stranglehold. You marvel at the steady nerve and the expertise of Botham and Edmonds as they continue to frustrate the West Indian. The fieldsmen are also rising to the occasion. Twice Dujon clips Botham firmly towards the umpire at square leg and both times Lamb, showing superb anticipation, dives full length to bring off sensational stops preventing even a single. The crowd, who are beginning to get behind this England side, roar their approval. Around the ground the bars are almost empty. The cricket is so absorbing that only the diehard drinkers remain. In the press box the journalists are unable to begin their match reports since there's no way that they can tell who is going to win this game. Radio 3 listeners are informed that commentary will continue right up until the conclusion of the match even if it lasts until eight o'clock and music lovers around the country groan.

In the middle Dujon is becoming a little desperate. In the forty-ninth over, bowled by Botham, he plays an agricultural heave and the ball balloons over mid-wicket for two. To the next delivery he plays an identical shot, swinging across the line of the ball, but this time he makes good contact and the ball speeds through mid-wicket for four; 202-5 in the 49th over. Clearly Dujon has decided to launch an assault and Botham asks for one of the leg-side fielders, who have been saving the single, to be placed on the mid-wicket boundary to stop him playing that shot. You agree that this is a good idea. You have a choice of two fielders. Should you send

A. Lamb? Or

B. Athey; to the deep-mid-wicket boundary?

If **A** turn to page 134
If **B** turn to page 136

A. Off the last ball of Botham's over Dujon plays a more orthodox clip through mid-wicket. On the boundary's edge Lamb has to sprint fifteen yards to his right. Border anxious to keep the strike for Edmonds's last over sets off for a second run. At the other end Dujon hesitates momentarily, but when he realises that Border is intent upon a second he starts running again. From extra cover you see that there is a chance of a run-out and you shout at the top of your voice 'Keeper's end' to Allan Lamb, who is concentrating on picking up the ball cleanly.

Once the ball is in his hand, Lamb throws it like a bullet straight to the top of the stumps and Paul Downton removes the bails triumphantly. It is one of David Shepherd's easier decisions; Dujon is a yard short of the crease and hardly bothers to look at the umpire before setting off for the pavilion.

Border is clearly frustrated by the needless loss of a wicket; his only consolation is that the new batsman is Roger Harper, who is not only an accomplished hitter but also one of the fastest runners playing cricket. Elsewhere on the square Lamb is apologising to Downton for his throw; he reckons it was six inches too high. Athey says that he used to be able to throw like that before his shoulder injury.

Edmonds's final over, the fiftieth of the innings, is a good one. Border is conscious that only four wickets remain and therefore plays a little more cautiously taking a single from the third ball and Harper is unable to get off the mark from the last three deliveries. The crowd applaud the end of Edmonds's spell and so do the players.

With the score standing at 203-6 the Rest of the World need to score 62 from the last ten overs to win the match. On air Fred Trueman points out without any assistance from Bill Frindall that the required run-rate is 6.2 per over.

Please turn to page 135

Of your three front-line bowlers Emburey has four overs left, Dilley and Botham three each. You decide that Emburey should bowl the 51st over at the Pavilion End since you reckon that it is too risky to have him bowling right at the very end of the innings and you warn Dilley that you would like him to bowl at the Nursery End.

By now Emburey's bowling bears little resemblance to the classical off-spin that was witnessed earlier in the innings. He is bowling at almost medium pace spearing the ball at the batsmen's feet, giving them no room to swing the bat. His main aim is the prevention of boundaries; at this stage of the game he doesn't mind conceding singles especially when Border is facing. Every 'dot' ball is applauded by the crowd with the same enthusiasm that greets a wicket maiden in a Test match.

Dilley meanwhile is steeling himself to maintain his concentration; he keeps his objectives very simple; he just aims to bowl fast and straight following the old-fashioned maxim of 'if they miss I hit'.

The fieldsmen are under the microscope as well; all are now prepared to strain every muscle in desperate dives along the boundary. A misfield or a dropped catch can change the course of the match now just as easily as a brilliant run-out.

The Border/Harper stand is becoming increasingly dangerous. In the fifty-third over Harper manages to get underneath one of Emburey's 'off-spinners' and the ball lands amongst the revellers in the Tavern, whilst Border is scoring off every ball he receives. However Dilley responds to the crisis by yorking the West Indian in the next over, during which he concedes just one run. 224-7 and Malcolm Marshall, a useful no. 9 by any standards, lopes to the wicket.

Emburey's penultimate over yields five runs, all from singles, leaving Marshall ready to face the bowling from the Nursery End. 229-7 from 55 overs. Who do you choose to bowl
A. Dilley? Or
B. Botham?

If **A** turn to page 138
If **B** turn to page 148

B. Off the last ball of Botham's over Dujon clips the ball through mid-wicket again. On the boundary Athey has to sprint fifteen yards to his right. Border anxious to be on strike for Edmonds's last over sets off for a second run. At the other end Dujon hesitates momentarily but once he sees that his captain is intent upon a second he starts running again. From extra cover you realise that there is a chance of a run-out and you bellow 'Keeper's end' to Athey who is concentrating on picking up the ball cleanly.

Once the ball is in his hand he throws it towards Paul Downton. As he lets go of the ball a piercing pain shoots along his shoulder-blade down to his elbow. His throw lacks power, which is hardly surprising considering that he hasn't thrown a ball in anger for eighteen months. The ball reaches Downton on the second bounce. He removes the bails more in hope than expectation and Umpire Shepherd confirms that Dujon has made his ground.

It is only now as Athey, clearly in agony, holds his right shoulder that you remember his nagging shoulder injury, to which the chairman had thoughtfully referred in his notes. If only you had remembered this earlier.

The sad truth is that this mistake has probably cost you a wicket. You make a mental note to keep Athey in the inner ring for the rest of the innings, hoping that this episode doesn't decide the outcome of the match. In the commentary box Trevor Bailey can't avoid the conclusion that placing Athey on the boundary was 'not a very sensible thing to do'.

Edmonds's final over, the fiftieth of the innings, yields four runs and the crowd applaud his spell. The score now stands at 207-5 with ten overs remaining. The Rest of the World need just 58 runs to win from the last ten overs. There's no doubt that at this stage they are the favourites.

Please turn to page 137

Now you decide that Emburey should bowl the 51st over from the Pavilion End since you don't think it a good idea that he should be bowling during the last two overs of the match. Dujon bisects long-on and deep mid-wicket with a lofted drive for four. However, attempting to repeat the shot off the last ball of the over he skies a catch to Botham on the leg-side boundary. 212-6 and a welcome opportunity to gather your thoughts. They need 53 from nine overs. Emburey, Dilley and Botham all have three overs left to bowl. As Harper strides to the wicket you decide that you are going to bowl Dilley from the Nursery End. So far he has looked the most penetrating of your seamers and you are desperate for another wicket.

Since the batsmen had crossed Dilley begins his spell to the tall, unsmiling West Indian, who fails to score off his first three balls, playing and missing at the first two. However Harper makes amends by slashing the fourth ball between third man and square cover for four and from the final ball he takes a single. A good over from Dilley and you applaud him. At the other end Emburey's bowling bears little resemblance to traditional off-spin. He is spearing the ball down as quickly as he can, aiming to pitch the ball on the batsman's toes so that he has no room to swing the bat. He manages to avoid conceding any boundaries but none the less six runs accrue from the 53rd over – and six runs per over is all they need.

Dilley now summons all his reserves of strength and succeeds in yorking Harper in the next over, during which he concedes just one run, a superb effort by the Worcestershire fast bowler who is now running up to the wicket like a rampaging Viking. 224-7 and Malcolm Marshall slowly makes his way to the wicket as the light begins to fade. Emburey's penultimate over yields five runs, all from singles, leaving Marshall ready to face the bowling from the Nursery End. 229-7 from 55 overs. Do you choose to bowl

A. Dilley? Or

B. Botham?

If **A** turn to page 138
If **B** turn to page 148

A. You toss the ball to Graham Dilley exhorting him to one last effort. 'You can do it,' you croak (your mouth is a little dry), though you realise that this is not so much a statement of fact, more an increasingly forlorn hope. On TV Ray Illingworth suggests that your decision to bowl Dilley out is either a very brave one or very foolish. It means that Ian Botham will not be able to complete his full quota of overs since there is now only room for him to bowl two of his three remaining overs; you'll have to find another over from someone else, presumably Graham Gooch. Dilley gives everything in his last over but is unable to make another breakthrough. Off the second ball Marshall scrambles a leg-bye and then Border, who has been in this situation many times before, calmly manipulates the ball to pick up three twos and a single. 237-7 with four overs remaining and the crowd applaud Dilley at the end of his spell. The gamble to bowl Dilley out (assuming it was a gamble rather than an oversight) hasn't worked and you are left with the problem of when to bowl Gooch.

You decide that Gooch will have to bowl the 59th over and whilst Emburey prepares for his last over you run over to tell him the good news.

'Thanks very much, skip' is his initial retort and he starts a series of loosening up exercises since he recognises that the situation won't really permit him to bowl any 'looseners' at the beginning of his spell. You recognise that you have put him into an unenviable position but there is really no alternative, short of bowling yourself. Bowling yourself? Now there's an idea. Roy of the Rovers always took the last-minute penalties in the comic strips of your youth. You remember reading somewhere that the great captains always lead from the front and take responsibility themselves. Perhaps you should bowl. This thought is tempered by a quote from Robertson-Glasgow that suddenly comes to mind. 'Cricket teams have often suffered from captains who have arrived, done queer things, departed and been forgotten.'

Turn to page 139

So there's plenty to think about as Emburey begins his last over, the 57th of the innings. The Rest of the World require 28 runs to win. Now every ball seems to take an age. After each single the field has to swap around since a left- and right-hander are at the crease and even then there are still adjustments to be made. Border takes a single to long-off from the first ball and you have to decide whether Emburey should have three or four men guarding the leg-side boundary, which seems to be getting shorter by the minute. You opt for three men in the deep on the leg side trying to put pressure on Marshall; this prompts the West Indian to swing the ball to leg and you wince when the ball crosses the rope. The extra fielder now goes out to the boundary.

Next ball Marshall drives the ball straight back to the bowler. No run.

'Well bowled, Embers. Come on, keep going,' you shout to no one in particular. You begin to realise how much you want to win this game. The last three balls of the over yield three singles. Emburey's job is done and the score is 245-7. Botham hands his sweater to David Shepherd. If ever there was a time for some Botham magic it is now. His first ball is short and not very fast. Marshall pulls ferociously and the ball flies through the air straight to mid-wicket where Athey takes a stinging catch. How does Botham get away with it? He laughs at his good fortune and does some loosening exercises as Abdul Qadir jauntily comes out to join Border. Botham's next ball is much quicker and to your delight Qadir misses it. However, they manage a leg-bye from the third. The field is now deep-set for Border, who drives the ball wide of long-off for an easy two; he repeats the shot next ball bringing two more runs and then he guides the last ball down to third man and sedately ambles a single to keep the strike. 251-8 with two overs remaining and Border is still in control. Now you must make your mind up. Are you going to expose yourself to the possibility of glorious success or spectacular failure? Do you bowl

A. Gooch? Or

B. yourself.

If **A** turn to page 143
If **B** turn to page 140

B. As Gooch makes his way to Dickie Bird at the Pavilion End you intercept him and tell him that there's been a change of plan. You are going to bowl. For a moment he is speechless; then he manages to splutter 'You're the captain' and he walks away.

It takes a long time to set your field; some of the players appear slow to react to your directions; maybe they are also in a state of shock. In the press box the typewriters have stopped tapping since even the most hardened of journalists is intrigued by your decision. In the commentary box Henry Blofeld admits to being 'absolutely flabbergasted'.

There is an eerie silence at Lord's as you run up to the wicket. Border taps his bat at the crease staring intently down the wicket. The ball is straight; he drives it back down the pitch firmly. You dive to your left and stop it; the crowd breaks into applause. Your second ball is wider; Border drives straight to David Gower at extra cover; no run. The Australian captain looks restless. He has dominated all the England bowlers so far, all proven international performers; surely he is not going to be humiliated by a complete unknown.

'Come on, skip; keep going' bellows Downton. The third ball is a little slower. Border swings with a hint of desperation and the ball goes twenty yards to Allan Lamb's right at deep mid-wicket. He sprints, dives full length and just manages to get his right hand under the ball, but as he hits the ground it bobbles out of his hand and over the boundary. The crowd groans; you bang your thigh in exasperation and stare up at the heavens. 255-8. If only that catch had stuck . . . It's not worth thinking about. Your fourth ball is short. Border cuts. Four runs. 259-8. Six to win. You feel a very lonely man as you run up to the wicket; no one can help you now. The ball is a fraction short. Border cuts and misses. No run. To the last ball of the over Border plays a powerful on-drive; the ball sails in the air towards John Emburey at long-on. With the manic urgency of a drowning man you scream, 'Catch it.'

Turn to page 142

Border square cuts and the run target is ever closer

The ball is caught, a remarkable catch for a seventy-five-year-old MCC member sitting outside the Long Room. Dickie Bird signals six as swiftly as possible, grabs the stumps and heads for the pavilion as the crowd begin to spill over on to the pitch.

Allan Border runs up to you and shakes your hand: 'Great game, mate. Thanks a lot.'

You are feeling dazed as the tension drains from your body. You just manage to utter a 'Well played' as he sprints past you anxious to avoid being buffeted by the crowd. You feel too exhausted to run; by now you are surrounded by spectators; some pat you on the back, others hurl abuse, but you don't really notice them.

Turn to page 170

A. You opt to bowl Gooch and in the commentary box Trevor Bailey points out that this is the 'sensible' thing to do in the circumstances. It takes a long time to sort out the field, but who cares about over-rate fines at this stage of the game? Finally you settle upon the following, bearing in mind that the left-handed Border is on strike. On the leg side there are three men on the boundary – long leg, square leg and long-on; the only fielder saving the single is a short mid-wicket. On the off side, down the slope, third man and deep square cover are on the boundary, whilst cover point, extra cover and mid-off are in the ring.

Border, who is seemingly unruffled by the delay, now settles into his stance as Gooch runs up to the wicket. He drives the ball straight to Emburey at mid-off who makes a fine stop. The batsmen think about running but reject the idea. The crowd applauds and Gooch plods back to his mark. Border clips the next ball off his legs wide of long leg. Without hesitating or even looking he turns for the second and just beats Dilley's throw. 253-8. Twelve to win. The third ball is driven to long-on's left; this time Qadir turns 'blind' and successfully scrambles a second, anxious to keep his captain on strike. 255-8. Border drives the next ball straight to Gower at extra cover. No run.

So far Gooch has conceded four runs from four balls, a fine effort since he is bowling at the Australian captain in full flow. You doubt whether you could have done any better yourself. The Rest of the World now need ten runs from eight balls as Gooch bowls the fifth ball of the over. Border steps down the wicket and lofts the ball over mid-off. He doesn't time the ball to perfection so Emburey gives chase but he's just unable to stop the ball from trickling up the slope in front of the pavilion. 259-8. One more shot like that and the game is virtually over. Do you decide

A. to leave Emburey on the long-off boundary? Or

B. to bring him back into the ring at mid-off?

If **A** turn to page 144
If **B** turn to page 146

A. 'No-ball,' yells David Shepherd from square leg as Gooch bowls the next delivery. This doesn't affect Border's shot, a drive wide of extra cover, which brings two more runs. With Emburey on the boundary, only three men remained in the ring and David Shepherd was left with no alternative but to call a no-ball. You are furious with yourself and your team-mates are none too happy either. This elementary error means that the game is now irretrievable since the score is now 261-8 and there are still seven balls left. On TV Illingworth in obvious anguish tries to remain restrained and merely points out that this is the sort of error that a professional captain would never make and he can't help questioning the wisdom of your original selection.

In the middle in despair you stare at your toes for a moment. Angrily you summon Emburey back into the ring and Gooch sets off with an air of resignation. Border turns the ball to long-leg for a single, thereby keeping the strike. 262-8.

Not even Botham can get you out of this pickle. His first ball is a little short and Border rocks on to the back foot and pulls triumphantly. The ball lands in the Mound Stand and is never returned. The little Australian quickly runs up to you and shakes your hand: 'Great game, mate. Thanks a lot.' Then he sprints for the pavilion to avoid being buffeted by the crowd who are now pouring over the boundary ropes. There's no time for you to reply, not that you can think of anything to say anyway.

Turn to page 170

As the match draws to a close, Botham requests a field change

B. You summon Emburey back into the ring at mid-off. Much as you might like to have a long-off it is imperative that you keep four men in the ring and you accept that you can't cover every possibility. You are relieved, to say the least, when Border drives the last ball of the over straight to Emburey and there's no run. 259-8. You are still in the game – just. Some of the players applaud Gooch's over, a stout effort in the circumstances but you have too many other things to think about as Botham hands his sweater to David Shepherd for the last time. The Rest of the World require six to win, but what if the scores are tied after sixty overs? You are glad you've thought of that. Now you interrogate David Shepherd who tells you that in the event of a tie the side losing fewer wickets shall be adjudged the winners. If the same number of wickets have been taken, then the side with the faster run-rate over the first thirty overs of their innings will win the game. So in effect with eight wickets down the Rest of the World need only five to win at the beginning of the last over. One consolation is that Qadir is on strike. Admittedly he is a dangerous hitter, but up until now Border has manipulated the bowling so well that he's hardly had to face a ball. Botham is about to bowl at the Nursery End with the famous slope running down to the Tavern and he announces that he intends to bowl straight. He assures you that if 'he misses, I'll hit, skip'. Predictably Botham still senses a good chance of winning this match. It is up to you to set the field. You narrow your choices down to two possible field settings.

A. On the off side a third man and a deep square cover on the boundary; cover point, extra cover and mid-off in the ring saving the single. On the leg side a long leg, a deep square leg and a long-on on the boundary and a short mid-wicket saving the single.

B. On the off side the same as above. On the leg side just a long leg on the boundary with a ring of three fielders, square leg, mid-wicket and mid-on saving the single.

If **A** turn to page 163
If **B** turn to page 152

A

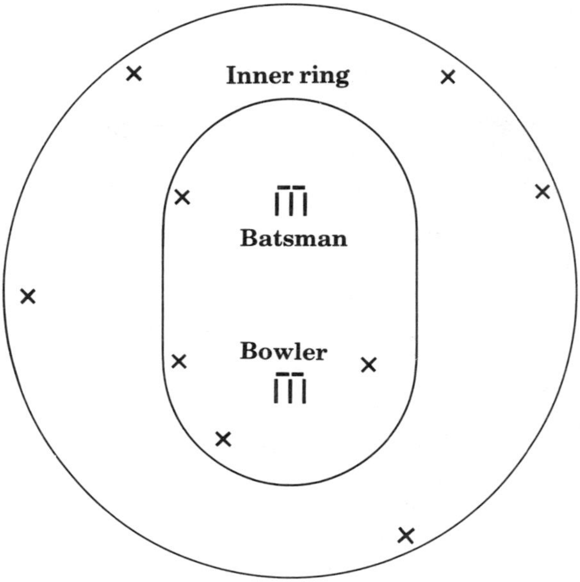

B

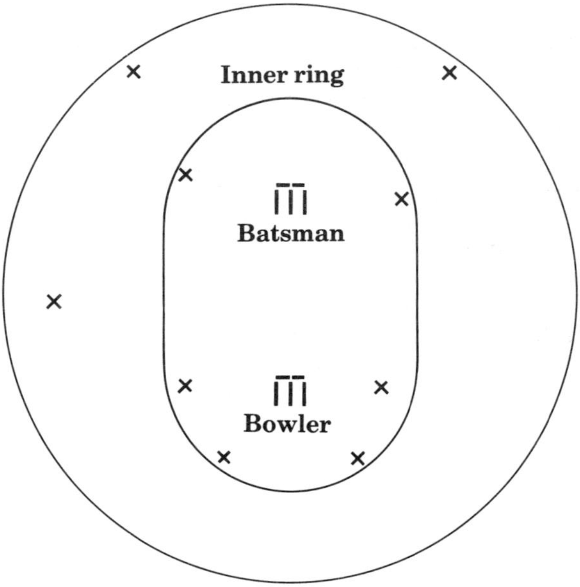

B. You summon Botham to the Nursery End. Ray Illingworth observes that this is a sound decision; if you hadn't opted to bowl Botham now he would not have been able to complete his quota of twelve overs so you would have been compelled to find an over from a non-specialist bowler, which is a highly undesirable state of affairs at the end of a limited-overs match. In the commentary box Trevor Bailey notes that your bowling change is 'eminently sensible'.

Botham's over, the 56th of the innings, yields six runs, all from scrambled singles, taking the score to 235-7. 'Well bowled' you shout since the Rest of the World now require more than a run a ball. To be precise they need 30 runs from four overs.

At the Pavilion End Emburey's final over maintains the pressure. By fizzing the ball right up into the block-hole he stops the batsmen hitting any boundaries and it is clear that Marshall in particular is becoming increasingly frustrated. Six more runs are added and the crowd give the local off-spinner a warm round of applause as he takes his sweater for the last time. 241-7.

Now Botham continues to torment Marshall. Having conceded just four runs from five balls, Botham induces the West Indian to swing wildly and the ball balloons to deep square leg where Lamb judges the catch perfectly. 245-8 and, as Qadir walks to the wicket, you consult with Dilley, who is to bowl the penultimate over of the match.

Fortunately Qadir is on strike since the batsmen had crossed whilst the ball was in the air. The little leg-spinner takes guard and fidgets nervously as he surveys the field, before settling into his stance. He gropes at Dilley's first ball and misses; he can't hide his anguish. Border comes down the wicket to offer advice and encouragement, no doubt suggesting that it would be a good idea if he could monopolise the strike.

Turn to page 149

The second ball raps Qadir on the pad; there's a loud appeal, whilst the batsmen set off for a run. Dickie Bird signals a leg-bye. 246-8. Border, the danger man, is now on strike. If you can prevent him from hitting boundaries the match is surely yours. Accordingly you take a long time to set the field. At the top end of the slope you have four fielders on the leg side; you have two men on the boundary at square leg and long-on. You bring fine leg up into the ring along with your mid-wicket. On the off side you have third man, deep cover and long-off on the boundary; in the ring Gower is at extra cover and you are at cover point. It seems sensible to have the extra fielder down the slope.

Now the tension finally seems to have affected the Australian since he swings desperately at the next ball, which passes harmlessly through to Downton, who immediately bellows his approval. No run. The score remains 246-8. Illingworth declares that you are now clear favourites to win the match.

Dilley runs in to bowl the fourth ball of the over; as he delivers, Border steps away to leg and slices the ball over your head at cover point for four runs. You trot down to the Mound Stand to retrieve it, wondering whether this highly effective shot was intentional or not. 250-8 with two balls remaining in Dilley's over.

The Worcester fast bowler sprints up to the wicket again and Border employs the same tactics with the same result. You are fuming as you go to fetch the ball. Two balls earlier the match seemed safe. With the score now at 254-8 it is wide open again. Your hard-won advantage is being frittered away. Angrily you scoop the ball up from beyond the boundary rope and hurl it back to the middle. Do you opt

A. to stay on the boundary at backward point, where the last two shots have ended up? Or

B. do you return to your original position at orthodox cover point?

If **A** turn to page 150
If **B** turn to page 161

A. Still fuming you opt to stay on the boundary. Dilley bowls again, but this time Border fails to make contact. Acute relief turns to deep despair when you spot the square-leg umpire, Shepherd, facing the scorers signalling a no-ball. With you on the boundary there were only three men in the ring. Your colleagues stare angrily in your direction as if to say, 'What the hell are you doing out there?' 255-8.

The last ball of the over is a poor one, pitching outside leg stump. Border, his confidence now restored, calmly plays a delicate leg glance and the ball races down to the fine-leg boundary. 259-8. You are no longer the favourites. Now you must steel yourself for the last over; there's no point in mulling over your mistake, at least not until after the game. The Rest of the World require six to win, but what if the scores are tied after sixty overs? You're glad you thought of that. You interrogate David Shepherd, who tells you that in the event of a tie the side losing the fewer wickets will be the winners. So in effect, with eight wickets down, the Rest of the World need only five to win at the beginning of the last over. One consolation is that Qadir is on strike. Admittedly he is a dangerous hitter but up until now Border has manipulated the bowling so that he's hardly had to face a ball.

Botham hands his sweater to David Shepherd at the Nursery End and announces that he intends to bowl straight. He assures you that 'if he misses I'll hit, skip'. It is up to you to set the field. You narrow your choices down to two possible field settings.

A. On the off side a third man and a deep square cover on the boundary; cover point, extra cover and mid-off in the ring saving the single. On the leg side a long leg, a deep square leg and a long-on on the boundary and just a short mid-wicket saving the single.

B. On the off side the same as above. On the leg side just a long leg on the boundary with a ring of three fielders, square leg, mid-wicket and mid-on saving the single.

If you choose **A** turn to page 163
If you choose **B** turn to page 152

Graham Dilley – brought back for the final overs

B. You conclude that you must keep Qadir on strike if you are going to win the game and so opt to have six fielders in the ring saving the single. The crowd roars as Botham gallops up to the wicket. Qadir drives the ball straight to mid-on and starts running down the wicket. Border sends him back immediately as Emburey's throw speeds towards Downton with unerring accuracy. The wicket-keeper appeals as Qadir scrambles to make his ground.

'Not out' shouts Dickie Bird. The action-replay machine in the TV studio confirms that Qadir was in by the narrowest of margins and on air Richie Benaud makes a point of commenting on the quality of the umpire's decision. What sane man would want to be an umpire in this situation? What sane man would want to be captain for that matter?

Botham runs in again. This time Qadir swings like a true tail-ender. He fails to make contact and the ball misses the off stump by a whisker. Botham holds his head in anguish. If Qadir misses, he had promised to hit and it had been so close. Still you're hardly in a position to complain since Botham has bowled two balls without conceding a run. The score still stands at 259-8 with four balls of the match remaining and Qadir is now becoming increasingly restless. Border goes down the wicket to chat to his partner; you can only speculate about what he's saying. Six runs are still needed to win the game, five to tie.

Whilst the two batsmen are huddled together in the middle you join Botham from mid-off as he slowly moves back to his mark. You realise that Qadir is quite likely to swing indiscriminately at the next ball even though Border may have told him just to push and run. Now at least there's more than a glimmer of hope for England. The question is

A. do you put your mid-on back to long-on and send your square leg out to the boundary, keeping the minimum of four fieldsmen in the ring? Or

B. do you keep the same field?

If **A** turn to page 157
If **B** turn to page 154

Downton breaks the stumps and awaits Dickie Bird's decision

B. You decide to keep six fielders in the ring to save the single, gambling on Qadir's inability to pierce the field. On TV Ray Illingworth suggests that this is a brave move since one good blow from Qadir could seal the match. Botham slowly retreats to his mark; he's taking his time now; he wants to keep Qadir on tenterhooks for as long as possible. At mid-off your hands are distinctly moist and you wipe them on your flannels as you move in. You don't want to drop a skier now. The roar of the crowd becomes more deafening with every stride that Botham takes. Botham bowls and Qadir drives, making good contact. The ball speeds to David Gower, who is very close at extra cover. There is no chance of a run as he makes a clean stop. The crowd is jubilant. At the non-striker's end Border is clearly distraught since he realises that the victory which seemed so likely at the beginning of the over is becoming increasingly difficult to achieve especially since he's been stranded at the non-striker's end for three balls.

Border and Qadir convene again in the middle of the wicket; Qadir is clearly frustrated and feels aggrieved that such a crisp shot had met with no reward. You go over to Botham to plan the next delivery. The score still stands at 259-8. Six to win, five to tie and three balls to go. In the commentary box Christopher Martin-Jenkins suggests that England are now favourites to win the match for the first time in a dozen overs but, not wanting to tempt fate, he stresses that it's still anyone's game. He sips a glass of water and prepares to relay the final three balls to his listeners.

In the middle you examine your field. At the moment there are still six fielders in the ring. With three balls remaining do you

A. send your square leg to the boundary and put your mid-on back to long-on? Or

B. keep the same field?

If **A** turn to page 156
If **B** turn to page 167

Botham prepares to bowl the last ball of the match

A. Once the two extra boundary fielders are in position, Botham bounds in once more. Qadir swings desperately and the ball flies to long-on where Emburey fields safely. One run. It was too much to expect Botham to bowl a maiden in the 60th over of the innings. The score is now 260-8 with two balls left. Assuming they don't lose any more wickets the Rest of the World require four runs to win the match.

To Border you keep the minimum of four fielders in the ring though you ensure that they stay right on the edge of the circle. You bring long leg up too so that you can have both mid-on and mid-off on the boundary. You urge all the boundary fielders to try to save two, though it is doubtful whether many of them can hear you, above the noise of the crowd.

Botham bounds in once more. Border heaves the ball to long-on's left. Gooch rushes towards it and returns the ball as swiftly as he can to Botham but he is unable to prevent Qadir completing the second run. With one ball remaining the Rest of the World require two runs to level the scores and therefore win the match. After eight hours of intense effort everything hinges on this last ball.

You trot over to Botham from cover point and the crowd grows silent, steeling themselves for the last ball. All the English fielders are doing the same.

'Ian, old bean, try not to bowl a no-ball.'

You run back to cover point. Botham reaches the end of his run-up, breathes in deeply and sets off. Border taps his bat in the crease, moves on to the front foot and drives the ball firmly straight to Emburey at long-off. Qadir immediately scampers towards the striker's end, turns as fast as he can and heads for home. At long-off Emburey gathers the ball and sends in a low skimming throw to Botham who is behind the stumps at the bowler's end. Qadir dives desperately as Botham removes the bails and appeals to the umpire, who is perfectly positioned. All at Lord's fix their eyes upon David Shepherd.

Please turn to page 159

A. Hedging your bets you send Emburey to long-on and Lamb to deep square leg since you reckon that there's a good chance that Qadir will be able to clear the infield at the third attempt. Botham charges in again and Qadir drives the ball along the ground to Emburey at long-on. One run. 260-8. Three balls remaining. If you can restrict the Rest of the World to a run a ball the match is yours. It's a big 'If'. The field changes over for Border; you bring long leg to the edge of the circle allowing both mid-on and mid-off to retreat to the boundary. From cover point you exhort all your fielders to try to save two, but it is doubtful whether they can hear you above the crowd. Now Botham attempts to bowl a yorker. However, Border manages to hit it on the full toss and the ball races away to Gooch's left at long-on. Qadir turns blind anxious to let Border retain the strike. As Gooch hurls the ball to the bowler's end the Pakistani dives desperately. Botham whips off the bails and appeals but David Shepherd confirms that he has made his ground. 262-8 with two balls to go. Unless a wicket falls they need just two runs to win the match. Now you decide to bring your boundary fielders in to save the single. You realise that Border is quite likely to penetrate them but there really is no alternative. Up in the Warner Stand Ray Illingworth agrees but adds that if he were a betting man he would put his money on the batting side. In the middle you shout for one last effort as Botham sets off. He bowls – short – and Border cuts. The ball fizzes to your right at cover point. You dive full length and stop the ball as the batsmen scamper a single. At least the match is still alive. 263-8. Qadir has to score a single to win the match. Now you run over to Botham. He suggests bowling a slower ball. Someone else thinks that you should have one fielder in the deep at mid-wicket since Qadir is likely to hole out having a slog. It is up to you. Do you instruct Botham to bowl

A. a slower ball? Or

B. fast and straight?

Should you have

C. a deep mid-wicket? Or

D. everyone saving the single?

If you choose **A** and **C** turn to page 158
If you choose **A** and **D** turn to page 160
If you choose **B** and **C** turn to page 162
If you choose **B** and **D** turn to page 164

A and C. Botham's slower ball has met with no more than sporadic success over the years but you decide to trust his instincts. You also take up the idea of a deep mid-wicket. If by any chance Qadir were to hole out to the lone boundary fielder there's no doubt that you will be a national hero in ninety seconds' time. You send one of your most reliable fielders, Allan Lamb, out to the boundary. There he receives a few jeers from the crowd, who have yet to grasp the subtlety of the move: 'You can't save the single from there.'

Abdul Qadir surveys the field carefully. He pays special attention to the deep mid-wicket as he ponders his tactics. At cover point you dry your sweaty hands on your flannels as Botham charges in, blatantly disguising his intention to bowl a slower ball. The ball loops gently down the wicket. Qadir rocks on to the front foot, pauses and then takes a step back and pulls the ball between the ring of leg-side fielders. It speeds to mid-wicket bouncing several times before reaching Allan Lamb. The spectators are right; he can't save the single and they waste no time yelling 'Told you'.

The batsmen don't try to attempt a second run. With the scores level the Rest of the World win the game since they have lost one wicket less. The tension drains from your body and suddenly you feel completely exhausted. After all that effort you are denied a famous victory off the last ball of the match. Qadir does a jig of celebration now that the torment of the final over is finished. Border is no less delighted, but remains more restrained. He runs over to you and shakes your hand: 'Thanks for the game, mate.'

Before you can conjure up a reply he is gone, anxious to avoid being buffeted by the crowd who are now spilling over the ropes in thousands. Soon you are engulfed by spectators; some pat you on the back, others hurl abuse but in your dazed state you don't really notice them.

Turn to page 170

'That's not out.'

You cannot hide your despair and for a few moments you stare down at the grass, trying to come to terms with your disappointment. Whilst you are lost in your thoughts you feel a gentle tap on the shoulder. You look up to see David Gower with a wide grin spreading across his face. This puzzles you.

'What are you so cheerful about?'

'I suggest you have a look at Dickie Bird, skip.'

Turning to square leg you see the forlorn figure of Dickie Bird shouting 'Scorer, scorer'. His right hand is lodged on his right shoulder and at the top of his voice he's yelling 'One short, one short'.

Gower explains: 'Abdul failed to make his ground at the striker's end. He was so desperate to get back for the second run he was six inches adrift. Dickie, God bless him, spotted this. Well done skip, you've guided us to victory.' You have guided England to victory even if you were one of the last people on the field to recognise it.

In the commentary box Christopher Martin-Jenkins begins his summary:

> 'In the most dramatic of finishes England have defeated the Rest of the World by one run. The scores: England 264-9; the Rest of the World 263-8. In a sensational last over . . .'

You run over to Allan Border and shake his hand. There are no hard feelings from him; he has already clarified what has happened with Dickie Bird and he accepts the decision with dignity and acute disappointment.

'Well played, mate. Good game.' You wonder whether you could have managed as much if you had been in his situation.

Turn to page 171

A and **D.** Even though the slower ball has never been one of the most potent weapons in Botham's armoury, you decide to trust in his instincts. However, you reject the idea of a deep mid-wicket; you reason that your only realistic chance of winning the game is if you compel Qadir to try to slog the ball into the wide open spaces beyond the infield. A deep mid-wicket might persuade him not to have an almighty heave but to concentrate simply on hitting the ball, which is all he has to do to give his side the best chance of winning the game.

Before jogging over to cover point you have one last thought for Botham: 'Try not to bowl a no-ball, old bean.'

He smiles and slowly moves back to his mark and takes a deep breath. At cover point you notice that your hands are distinctly moist; you wipe them on your flannels. It is mildly reassuring to see several of your colleagues doing the same.

Lord's falls strangely silent as Botham charges in, doing his utmost to disguise his intention of bowling a slower ball. He bowls and the ball loops gently down the wicket. Qadir, eyes a-popping, swings. He swings far too early and from an outside edge the ball balloons up into the air to the left of cover point. It's your catch but you yell 'Mine' anyway; the shout suggests far more confidence than you actually feel. As you run backwards and to your left it seems as if the ball is attached to a yo-yo as it bobbles in front of your eyes. Finally you dive, a manoeuvre which seems to demand that you have your eyes shut. When you open them you find that the ball is safely lodged in your hands.

Within seconds you are surrounded by ecstatic team-mates. Botham treats you to one of his bear hugs. Once you have recovered your breath, you run over to shake Border's hand. Without trying to mask his disappointment he says, 'Well played, mate. Good game.' By now the spectators have spilled over the ropes and it takes a while to reach the pavilion steps where a standing ovation greets you as you lead England off the field.

Turn to page 171

B. You run back into the ring, conscious that however much you would like another boundary fielder you must keep a minimum of four fielders in the ring. Dilley sets off to bowl the last ball of his spell. Again Border steps away to leg but this time Dilley spears the ball in at his feet. You are relieved when he fails to make contact, though you would have been happier still if the ball had clipped the leg stump. Botham now strides up and hands his sweater to the umpire for the last time. The score is 254-8 so the Rest of the World require eleven runs to win the match, but what if the scores are tied? You're glad you've thought of that. Now you interrogate David Shepherd who tells you that in the event of a tie the side losing fewer wickets shall be the winners. If the same number of wickets have been taken then the side with the faster run-rate over the first thirty overs of their innings will win the game. So, in effect, with eight wickets down, the Rest of the World need ten to win the match at the beginning of the over.

After a consultation with your bowler you decide to keep just the four fielders in the ring to Qadir. He's a capable slogger and boundaries must be prevented at all costs. Botham announces that he intends to bowl straight and fast – 'If they miss I'll hit, skip'. At least he's confident. Botham bounds up to the wicket and bowls. Qadir swings and the next thing you see is the leg stump cartwheeling towards the keeper. You rush over to congratulate him. 254-9 with five balls left.

The Rest of the World's last batsman, Bruce Reid, now lopes to the wicket. He is not a particularly reassuring sight for captain Allan Border. He is a far more menacing figure with a ball in his hand than a bat. With the bright yellow helmet of Western Australia perched uncomfortably on the top of his head he looks like a flickering candle that could be extinguished by the faintest puff of wind. Border goes over to greet him and to issue instructions whilst you bring an extra man into the ring. A 'dot' ball now would be invaluable.

Turn to page 165

B and **C**. You impose your veto on the idea of Botham's slower ball since you reckon that this is no time for a whimsical experiment. Anyway Botham's slower ball has met with limited success over the years; it is on a par with Edmonds's wrist-spinners.

'Fast and straight, please, Ian.' He nods and walks slowly back to his mark taking several deep breaths on the way.

However, you like the idea of having one lone fielder on the boundary and you send one of your most reliable men, Allan Lamb, out to the mid-wicket boundary. At cover point you dry your perspiring hands on your flannels as Botham charges in to bowl the last ball of the match. He hurls the ball down with all his might. It is fast and straight, just as you ordered. Qadir swings; the ball clips the outside edge of his bat and Downton dives to his right. However, the dive is more a final gesture of defiance than a realistic attempt to catch the ball which speeds down to the untenanted third-man boundary. No one contemplates chasing it. There's no point. In the commentary box Chris Martin-Jenkins relays the news to cricket-lovers around the country – and a few frustrated music-lovers.

> In a dramatic finish the Rest of the World have defeated England by two wickets. The scores: England 264-9. The Rest of the World 267-8. In a sensational last over . . .

The tension drains from your body and suddenly you feel completely exhausted. After all that effort you are denied a famous victory off the last ball of the match. Qadir does a jig of celebration now that the torment of the final over is finished. Border is no less delighted, but remains more restrained. He runs over to you and shakes your hand: 'Great game mate. Thanks a lot.'

Before you can conjure up a reply he is gone, anxious to avoid being buffeted by the crowd who are now spilling over the ropes in thousands. Soon you are engulfed by spectators; some pat you on the back, others hurl abuse but in your dazed state you don't really notice them.

Turn to page 170

A. In the commentary box Christopher Martin-Jenkins admits to being 'surprised' by your field placements, since the best chance of an English victory is surely if Qadir is kept on strike. That is going to be hard to achieve with just the minimum of four fielders in the ring.

Botham charges up to the wicket and keeps his promise, bowling the ball fast and straight. Qadir swings but succeeds only in getting an inside edge and the ball trickles towards square leg. Border immediately summons him for a run which is completed easily since the only fielder saving the single on the leg side is at mid-wicket. 260-8 with five balls remaining. The field changes around for the left-handed Border still with the four fielders in the ring. Botham now attempts to bowl a yorker, but the Australian captain manages to hit the ball on the full toss. It races to long-on's left, and Qadir anxious to stay away from the strike scrambles back to the bowler's end to complete the second run. 262-8 with four balls left. Now – belatedly – you bring all your fielders up to save the single and on TV Ray Illingworth can't avoid observing that it would have been better if you had adopted this policy at the beginning of the over when Qadir was on strike. It's too late now.

Botham's next ball is perfectly respectable – a good length, straight and reasonably fast but Border's eye is well and truly in. He puts his right leg down the wicket and swings the ball triumphantly to the mid-wicket boundary. The Rest of the World have won the match by two wickets. The tension drains from your body and suddenly you feel completely exhausted. Border smiles for the first time in several hours and runs over to you and shakes your hand: 'Well played, mate. Thanks a lot.'

Before you can conjure up a reply he is gone, anxious to avoid being buffeted by the crowd who are now spilling over the ropes in thousands. Soon you are engulfed by spectators; some pat you on the back, others hurl abuse but in your dazed state you don't really notice them.

Turn to page 170

B and **D.** You instruct Botham not to bowl his slower ball, deciding that this is scarcely the time for one of his whimsical experiments.

'Fast and straight please, Ian.'

He looks a trifle disappointed but nods his acceptance of your decision as he slowly walks back to his mark, taking several deep breaths as he goes. You opt to keep all your fielders in the ring, however. You want to encourage Qadir to swing wildly so you are prepared to leave plenty of wide open spaces beyond the infield.

At cover point you dry your perspiring hands on your flannels as Botham charges in to bowl the last ball of the match. He hurls the ball down with all his might. It is fast and straight, just as you ordered. Qadir swings; the ball clips the outside edge of his bat and Downton dives to his right. However the dive is more a final gesture of defiance than a realistic attempt to catch the ball which speeds down to the untenanted third-man boundary. No one contemplates chasing it. There's no point. In the commentary box Chris Martin-Jenkins relays the news to cricket-lovers around the country – and a few frustrated music-lovers.

> In a dramatic finish the Rest of the World have defeated England by two wickets. The scores: England 264-9. The Rest of the World 267-8. In a sensational last over . . .

The tension drains from your body and suddenly you feel completely exhausted. After all that effort you are denied a famous victory off the last ball of the match. Qadir does a jig of celebration now that the torment of the final over is finished. Border is no less delighted, but remains more restrained. He runs over to you and shakes your hand: 'Great game mate. Thanks a lot.'

Before you can conjure up a reply he is gone, anxious to avoid being buffeted by the crowd who are now spilling over the ropes in thousands. Soon you are engulfed by spectators; some pat you on the back, others hurl abuse but in your dazed state you don't really notice them.

Turn to page 170

Botham races in; Reid now surprises himself and his captain by playing a perfectly respectable on-drive which brings him one run to long-on. 255-9 with four balls to go. Much depends on Border now. You position your four fielders on the edge of the circle; the rest patrol the boundary anxiously.

Border charges the next ball, which is directed at his legs. He adjusts skilfully and clips the ball to leg with perfect timing. It bisects deep mid-wicket and square leg. Four runs. 259-9. Three balls to go. Botham walks slowly back to his mark breathing deeply as he goes. He turns and charges in once more. This time he bowls a yorker. It is a good one. Border can only squeeze the ball out to extra cover for a single. The crowd sighs with relief and so do you. 260-9. Two balls to go. Now the left-handed Reid is on strike. You decide to maintain a deep-set field, having been impressed by his first stroke. You must avoid a boundary at all costs. There are just the four fielders in the ring and from extra cover you instruct them to stay right on the edge of the circle thirty yards from the bat.

Botham rushes in and bowls. Reid attempts to drive but fails to middle the ball, which rolls gently towards you at extra cover. After a slight hesitation Reid sets off for a single; he is an ungainly runner and takes a while to reach top speed which isn't very fast anyway. At extra cover you sense that there is an outside chance of running Reid out at the bowler's end if you can effect a direct hit. Do you

A. pick up the ball and hurl it at the stumps at the bowler's end? Or

B. lob the ball to the wicket-keeper, thereby conceding the single?

If **A** turn to page 166
If **B** turn to page 169

A. You throw the ball with all your might. If you hit the wickets the match is over. You don't. You are six inches astray. Even worse the lone mid-wicket fieldsman is unable to move fast enough to prevent the ball speeding towards the boundary. He dives in vain. Suddenly you realise the implications of what you have done. Edmonds at long-on and Lamb who has been fielding at deep square leg both sprint at full speed in an effort to stop the ball crossing the boundary. Lamb is the quicker of the two but he has further to run. With the ball now feet from the rope they take off simultaneously. They collide with a crunch. As for the ball, it serenely crosses the rope, unaware of the carnage it has left behind. Umpire Shepherd now indicates to the scorers that five runs have been scored and pulls the stumps out of the ground. Border can't believe his luck and he rushes over to Reid, the unlikeliest of batting heroes. You are in a state of disbelief. Seconds earlier you had spotted an opportunity to win the game in the most glorious style. Now it is all over.

In the commentary box a breathless Christopher Martin-Jenkins relays the news to his listeners.

> In a dramatic finish the Rest of the World defeated England by one wicket. The scores: England 264-9 from their sixty overs; the Rest of the World 265-9. In a sensational last over . . .

The tension drains from your body and suddenly you feel completely exhausted. After all that effort you have literally thrown away a famous victory off the penultimate ball of the match. Border runs over to you and shakes your hand: 'Great game mate. Thanks a lot.'

Before you can conjure up a reply he is gone, anxious to avoid being buffeted by the crowd who are now spilling over the ropes in thousands. Soon you are engulfed by spectators; some pat you on the back, others hurl abuse but in your dazed state you don't really notice them.

Turn to page 170

B. Christopher Martin-Jenkins describes your decision to keep six fieldsmen in the ring as 'an extraordinarily brave one in the circumstances'. Botham rushes in and Qadir swings. This time he middles the ball, which skims over mid-on to the boundary. Umpire Shepherd signals four runs and the game has undoubtedly swayed decisively back into the Rest of the World's favour. 263-8. Now there are no choices left to you. You wave all the fielders into the circle. Botham bowls and Qadir misses. You are hanging on by your fingertips. One ball remains. At cover point you dry your perspiring hands on your flannels as Botham charges in to bowl the last ball of the match. He hurls the ball down with all his might. It is fast and straight, just as you ordered. Qadir swings; the ball clips the outside edge of his bat and Downton dives to his right. However, the dive is more a final gesture of defiance than a realistic attempt to catch the ball which speeds down to the untenanted third-man boundary. No one contemplates chasing it. There's no point. In the commentary box Chris Martin-Jenkins relays the news to cricket-lovers around the country – and a few frustrated music-lovers.

In a dramatic finish the Rest of the World have defeated England by two wickets. The scores: England 264-9. The Rest of the World 267-8. In a sensational last over . . .

The tension drains from your body and suddenly you feel completely exhausted. After all that effort you are denied a famous victory off the last ball of the match. Qadir does a jig of celebration now that the torment of the final over is finished. Border is no less delighted, but remains more restrained. He runs over to you and shakes your hand: 'Cheers, mate. Thanks a lot.'

Before you can conjure up a reply he is gone, anxious to avoid being buffeted by the crowd who are now spilling over the ropes in thousands. Soon you are engulfed by spectators; some pat you on the back, others hurl abuse but in your dazed state you don't really notice them.

Turn to page 170

Border contemplates the tight finish

B. You lob the ball to Paul Downton and the batsmen take a single; a fine time this would be to risk four overthrows and the 'keeper acknowledges your restraint. The score is now 261-9 with one ball left. Border has to hit a boundary to win the match. You run over to Botham to check the field. Every possible man is right on the boundary edge. The four in-fielders are instructed to stay right on the edge of the circle. Botham declares that he aims to bowl a fast, straight yorker and you wish him 'Good Luck'. Before running back to extra cover you offer one final thought: 'Ian, old bean, try not to bowl a no-ball.' He smiles and walks slowly back to his mark. After eight hours of intense competition the match is finally to be decided.

The crowd falls strangely silent as Botham charges in. Two seconds later they are in uproar and Botham and Border, arch-rivals, close friends, are arm in arm in the middle of the wicket. Border pauses for a moment and looks back at the stumps. The middle one is missing.

Up in the commentary box Christopher Martin-Jenkins relays the news to his listeners:

> Botham has bowled Border with the last ball of the match so England have defeated the Rest of the World by three runs. The scores: England 264-9. The Rest of the World 261 all out. In a sensational finish . . .

In the middle you run over to Border and shake him by the hand; though obviously bitterly disappointed he is gracious in defeat: 'Well played, mate. Good game.'

By now the spectators have spilled over the boundary ropes and it takes several minutes for you to reach the pavilion steps. Once you are there a standing ovation greets you as you lead England off the field.

Turn to page 171

Back in the dressing room you slump into a chair, drained and dejected. There are so many things that you wish you had done differently. Now they flood through your mind. You fully expect your team-mates to question some of the decisions you made and you are surprised when nobody does. They are clearly disappointed but there are no recriminations. Maybe they have come to recognise that a *post mortem*, no matter how heated or detailed, is not going to change the result of the match. This is not the time to examine what went wrong.

Finally Allan Lamb gets out of his chair and declares that it's time for a drink. He brings you a beer and offers Botham a slimline tonic. Botham tells him quite specifically what he can do with his slimline tonic. Gower quietly inquires whether there's any champagne and having failed to discover any declares that he's going to procure some from the other dressing room. The telephone rings; it's for Edmonds and gradually the dressing room returns to normal.

After a couple of beers you have sufficient energy to take yourself off for a long hot bath. You linger there for half an hour or so replaying some of the incidents of the day in your mind. When you return to the dressing room it is empty. You pack your bags and see a souvenir programme lying on the table; you slip it under your arm, take one last fleeting look at the debris in the dressing room and then depart.

Outside the Grace Gates there are still throngs of people. Three times you attempt to hail a taxi but each time you are ousted by an MCC member. You decide to take the tube and slowly walk the four hundred yards to St John's Wood Station. As you enter the station two young teenagers spot the souvenir programme under your arm: 'Been to the cricket have you? Was it a good game?'

A thousand possible responses rush through your mind, but finally you settle upon 'Yes, it was' before descending into the grey anonymity of St John's Wood Tube Station.

THE END

As you enter the dressing room the Chairman greets you with a wide smile and a firm handshake. Already the attendant has brought in half a dozen bottles of champagne. Botham immediately seizes one, uncorks it and proceeds to spray it at anyone within range. Gower more animated now than at any time in the day deplores such a waste and tells him so in no uncertain terms. There's a knock on the door and a voice: 'Captain, would you mind having a word with the press?'

Outside in the corridor there are twenty or thirty journalists all armed with pads and pens and you are confronted by a barrage of questions. You were a little surprised by your selection . . . 264 was a good score . . . Allan Border had given you several anxious moments . . . it was a brave innings . . . tremendous all-round team performance . . . a tremendous last over by Ian Botham . . . no, you can never write him off . . . that's up to the selectors isn't it?

Back in the dressing room the players are still celebrating. You are happy to join them. One by one they go off to shower. Many have long journeys to make and county sides anxious to have them back. Finally you decide upon a long hot bath. You close your eyes and relive some of the memorable moments of the match; you linger there for half an hour or so and when you return to the dressing room it is empty. You pack your bags, take one last took at the debris and depart.

Hours later you turn the front-door key and a familiar voice sings out from the sitting room.

'How's your day been?'

You make yourself comfortable in an armchair, pause for a moment's thought and then begin.

'Well, I got to the ground at 9.30 and the gateman – you'll never believe this . . .'

THE END

ABOUT THE AUTHORS

Vic Marks was educated at Blundell's School and St John's College, Oxford, where he read Classics. At Oxford he gained four cricket Blues and was captain for two seasons, in 1976 and 1977

He made his County debut for Somerset in 1975 and was awarded his County cap four years later. He made his first appearance for England in a one-day international against the West Indies at Lord's in 1980. Since then he has played in six Tests and 33 one-day internationals and has toured with England three times. He has also spent one season, 1986–87, with Western Australia.

Vic lives with his wife, Anna, and their two daughters Amy and Rosie, in Tiverton, Devon.

Robin Drake was born in Calcutta, India in 1949. He toured there with his parents more or less continuously until returning home to England, aged six. He was educated at the Dragon and St Edward's school, Oxford, and after an incomplete course in Medicine at Bristol University, undertook a variety of occupations before settling in industry.

He has made numerous Test and County appearances as a spectator, and made a name for himself with the sponsors at the 1987 NatWest final by losing his Access card. Known affectionately by his team mates as 'not picked', he has developed the lofted cover-drive over mid-wicket in limited overs league cricket as a device for attracting sympathy.

Robin also lives in Tiverton, with his wife Wendy and three daughters, Joanna, Emily and Jessica.